PostSecret

EXTRAORDINARY CONFESSIONS

PostSecret

FROM ORDINARY LIVES

compiled by **FrankWarren**

An Orion paperback

First published in Great Britain in 2006
by Orion
This edition published in 2008
by Orion Books Ltd,
Orion House, 5 Upper St Martin's Lane,
London WC2H 9EA

An Hachette UK company

10 9 8 7 6 5

A CIP catalogue record for this book is available from the British Library.

ISBN 978-0-7528-8306-9

Printed and bound in Spain by Cayfosa (Impresia Ibérica)

The Orion Publishing Group's policy is to use papers that are natural, renewable and recyclable products and
made from wood grown in sustainable forests. The logging and manufacturing processes are expected to conform to
the environmental regulations of the country of origin.

www.orionbooks.co.uk

This book is dedicated to every person who faced their secret on a postcard, released it into a mailbox, and bravely shared it with me, the world, and themselves.

—Frank

The Most Trusted Stranger in America

I met Frank Warren after seeing PostSecret at Artomatic—a Washington, D.C., arts festival. As a practicing clinical psychologist and art gallery owner with an eye toward the psychological and healing aspects of art, I was looking for new artists to show at my gallery. At the PostSecret installation, I saw three rows of postcards, each with a taboo thought, each with artistic images, carefully clipped to display wires. There hung dozens of anonymous secrets on public display.

"This is one of the most amazing projects I have ever seen," I said to my husband. "I've got to have this in the gallery." Without pausing, my husband looked at me with worry. "Do you think the person who is doing this is safe?" he asked.

Frank, it turns out, is very safe. A father, husband, and business owner, he has no formal art background or training and refers to himself as an "accidental artist." Four years ago Frank experienced an emotional crisis in his life. Developing a passion for postcard art projects was how he worked through it. It became his personal experience of healing through art. He doesn't like to think too much about the origin or meanings of his postcard art works. He likens it to trying to understand why a joke is funny; the magic may be lost in the attempt to analyze it. He does know this: While at camp, when he was nine years old, he wrote a postcard to his family. He arrived home before the card did. Receiving it seemed magical and felt deeply meaningful to him. He had intercepted a message from himself as he had been days earlier. As he considers the event now, he believes those themes of home, understanding our changing identities, and self-communication held long-term inspiration.

Why is PostSecret so appealing? It is because Frank has tapped into the universal stuff of being human—the collective, often unconscious level of existence that defies age, culture, gender, economics, and so on. From this universal level come great and timeless works of art: theater, music, dance, visual art, and literature. At this universal level lie the depths of spirituality: mythological tales, sacred text, and ritual. Also from this universal level comes direct access to healing and personal transformation. Although in Western cultures we act as though there is a separation, there is no separation of the arts from spirituality or healing.

By participating in PostSecret, we all are invited into that collective level to become artists—free to explore and share private aspects of ourselves creatively, both through writing and through the alternative language of visual art. Whether we are PostSecret creators or viewers, we are affected and changed by experiencing the creative process and interacting with the resulting works of art.

The project also invites us into the collective level to heal ourselves, healing that has several characteristics similar to psychotherapy. For example, the prominent themes in PostSecret mirror some of the reasons people are drawn to psychotherapy: seeking relief from suffering; sharing painful experiences (especially concerning difficulties in relationships or feelings of isolation); expressing shame and anxiety about aspects of self that are difficult to face; and admitting one's impulses, fears, and fantasies. Although many of the secrets are about psychological pain, the grist for the mill in psychotherapy, others are hopeful, optimistic, or even humorous. Hope and humor are certainly important aspects of the psychotherapeutic process as well.

In PostSecret, by being asked to share a secret, we are invited to journey into our depths, perhaps into the unconscious mind, beneath the level of our awareness at the moment. Perhaps we venture into the preconscious where our secrets are already on the verge of awareness and emergence, or maybe into the conscious, where our secrets are being held back, ready to be let out under the right circumstances. As in psychotherapy, we are provided with a projective screen onto which anything can be placed and viewed. In this case, it is the postcard.

Also, as in psychotherapy, there is an action element in PostSecret. There is something that we can do—fill out the postcard. Reading the postcards is also a form of taking action. Something might change. There is hope. My patients often tell me how much better they feel after making the phone call to arrange for the first therapy appointment or after the first psychotherapy session. They have taken action toward healing; they feel hopeful that their lives will improve.

Both in psychotherapy and in PostSecret, the goal is to bring experience to conscious awareness and to express what is deepest inside and not have it be the end of the world. The goal is to make inner experience concrete by placing it outside the self. This exercise gives us the potential and the opportunity for self-reflection, for self-acceptance, for increased understanding about the self, and for healing and personal growth.

PostSecret is even briefer than the briefest of psychotherapies. The healing experience in PostSecret is bite-size, manageable. One postcard, one shared aspect of self, the secret, shared in a structured way, shared as part of an art project that may slip quietly under the radar of the psychological defenses. Release the secret onto the card, then release the card to Frank by mailing it, and notice what happens inside.

Albeit an anonymous process, PostSecret also shares some characteristics of the healing relationship with psychotherapy. At the foundation of psychotherapy is relationship, no matter the technique. It is about one human being expressing authentic caring and concern for another, offering comfort, witness, acceptance, assistance, and hope. When you send the postcard to Frank, he is on the other end to receive it. The same person who has offered us an opportunity to share has taken an interest in us and is there for us, unconditionally.

In PostSecret, art and healing are one, brilliantly condensed into the elegant simplicity of filling out a postcard. All for the price of a 37-cent stamp.

Frank told me recently, "There are times when I feel like this project has chosen me and not the other way around, and at times it feels like it may have picked the wrong person." Or maybe it has found exactly the right person.

Anne C. Fisher, Ph.D.
August 2005

Anne C. Fisher is a former classical ballerina, a practicing dance therapist, and a clinical psychologist.
The Anne C. Fisher Fine Art Gallery is located in Georgetown in Washington, D.C.

SHARE A SECRET

You are invited to anonymously contribute a secret to a group art project. Your secret can be a regret, fear, betrayal, desire, confession or childhood humiliation. Reveal *anything* - as long as it is true and you have never shared it with anyone before.

Steps:
Take a postcard, or two.
Tell your secret anonymously.
Stamp and mail the postcard.

Tips:
Be brief – the fewer words used the better.
Be legible – use big, clear and bold lettering.
Be creative – let the postcard be your canvas.

SEE A SECRET
www.postsecret.com

PostSecret
13345 Copper Ridge Rd
Germantown, Maryland
20874-3454

INTRODUCTION

In November 2004, I printed 3,000 postcards inviting people to share a secret with me: something that was true, something they had never told anyone. I handed out these cards at subway stations, I left them in art galleries, and I slipped them between the pages of library books. Then, slowly, secrets began to find their way to my mailbox.

After several weeks I stopped passing out postcards but secrets kept coming. Homemade postcards made from cardboard, old photographs, wedding invitations, and other personal items artfully decorated arrived from all over the world. Some of the secrets were written in Portuguese, French, German, Hebrew, and even Braille.

One of the first PostSecrets I received looked like nothing more than a worn postcard filled with two shopping lists. But squeezed into the corner was a soulful admission, "I am still struggling with what I've become."

Like fingerprints, no two secrets are identical, but every secret has a story behind it. From the clues on this card, I imagined that this person had an internal struggle about sharing the secret. It was so difficult that they tried to use up the postcard as a shopping list, twice. But the urge to reconcile with a painful personal truth was so strong that they were ultimately able to find the courage to share it.

Secrets have stories; they can also offer truths. After seeing thousands of secrets, I understand that sometimes when we believe we are keeping a secret, that secret is actually keeping us. A New Zealander recently wrote the following about what they had learned from the PostSecret project: "The things that make us feel so abnormal are actually the things that make us all the same."

I invite you to contemplate each of the shared secrets in these pages: to imagine the stories behind the personal revelations and to search for the meaning they hold. As you read these postcards you may not only be surprised by what you learn about others, but also reminded of your own secrets that have been hiding. That is what happened to me.

After reading one particular PostSecret, I was reminded of a childhood humiliation—something that happened to me more than thirty years ago. I never thought of it as a secret, yet I had never told anyone about it. From a memory that felt fresh, I chose my words carefully and expressed my secret on a postcard. I shared it with my wife and daughter. The next day, I went to the post office, and physically let it go into a mailbox. I walked away feeling lighter.

I like to think that this project germinated from that secret I kept buried for most of my life. At a level below my awareness, I needed to share it, but I was not brave enough to do it alone. So I found myself inviting others at galleries and libraries to first share their secrets with me. And when their postcards found me, I was able to find the courage to identify my secret and share it too.

We all have secrets: fears, regrets, hopes, beliefs, fantasies, betrayals, humiliations. We may not always recognize them but they are part of us—like the dreams we can't always recall in the morning light.

Some of the most beautiful postcards in this collection came from very painful feelings and memories. I believe that each one of us has the ability to discover, share, and grow our own dark secrets into something meaningful and beautiful.

—Frank

i don't know WHICH ONE
to send in.

Post secret
13345 Lopper Ridge Rd.
Germantown, MD
20874-3454

I can't think of a secret.
Except—
I don't think I'm interesting
                    enough to
                 have
              a
           secret.

POSTSECRET
13345 COPPERRIDGE RD
GERMANTOWN,
              MARYLAND
    USA 20874-3454

20874/3454

17

I found these
stamps →
as a child, and I

have been
waiting all my
life to have someone
to send them to.
I never did have
someone.

Conestoga Wagon 1800s 3 USA
Conestoga Wagon 1800s USA 3
Conestoga Wagon 1800s USA 3
Conestoga Wagon 1800s USA 3
Conestoga Wagon 1800s USA 3
Conestoga Wagon 1800s USA 3
Conestoga Wagon 1800s USA 3
Locomotive 1870s 2 USA

Post Secret
13345 Copper Ridge Rd
Germantown, MD
     20874-3454

R046

20

I know
You don't really
like me.
(please stop pretending)

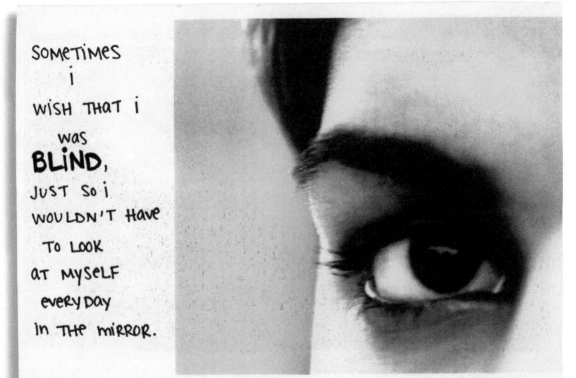

SOMETIMES
i
WISH THAT i
WAS
BLiND,
JUST SO i
WOULDN'T HAVE
TO LOOK
AT MYSELF
EVERY DAY
iN THE MiRROR.

When I'm alone I see myself as beautiful.

It's when I'm around others that I feel so UGLY & FLAWED.

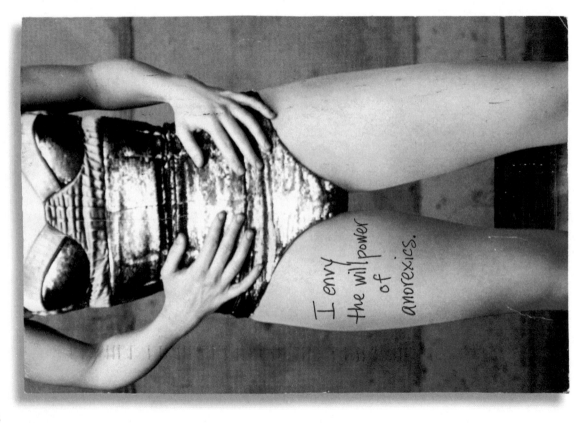

sometimes

I PUT COINS IN
OTHER PEOPLE'S
PARKING METERS

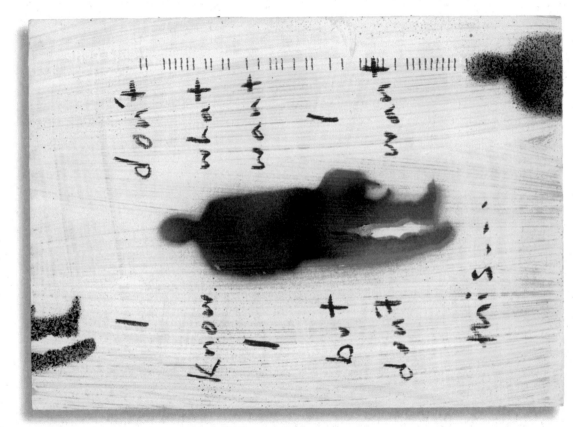

28

"There are two kinds of secrets: those we keep from others and the ones we hide from ourselves."

—Frank

When I was in the Fourth Grade, a new kid moved into our neighborhood.

He was a charismatic leader who quickly became popular.

Soon after, he convinced two of my friends to pin me to the ground and hold open my eyelids.

They took turns spitting into my eyes.

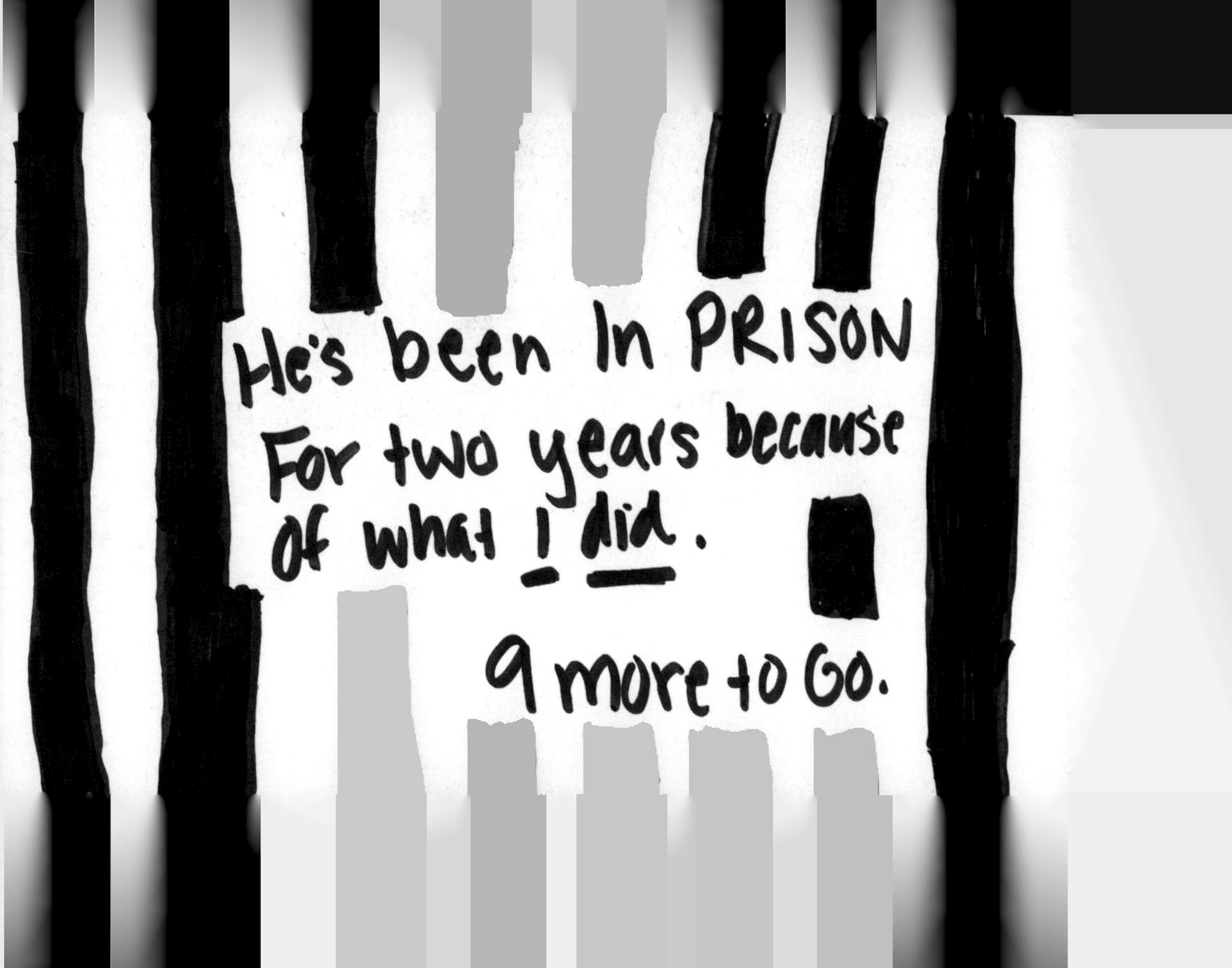
He's been In PRISON
For two years because
of what I did.
9 more to Go.

PEOPLE THINK I'VE STOPPED LYING ... but I've just gotten better at it

I AM HOME-
LESS AND
NO ONE
(NOT EVEN
MY FAMILY)
KNOWS ABOUT IT.

34

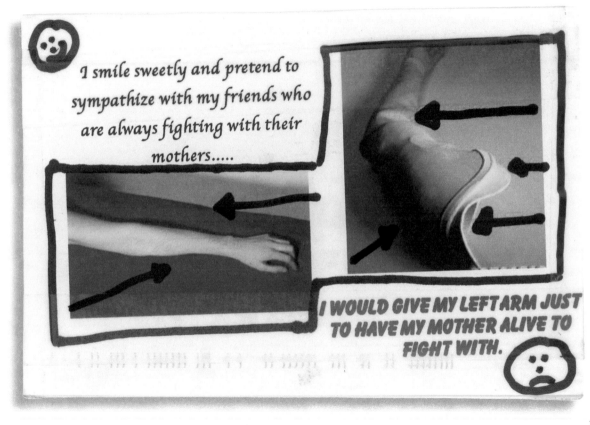

I smile sweetly and pretend to sympathize with my friends who are always fighting with their mothers.....

I WOULD GIVE MY LEFT ARM JUST TO HAVE MY MOTHER ALIVE TO FIGHT WITH.

I'm
JEALOUS
of her baby...

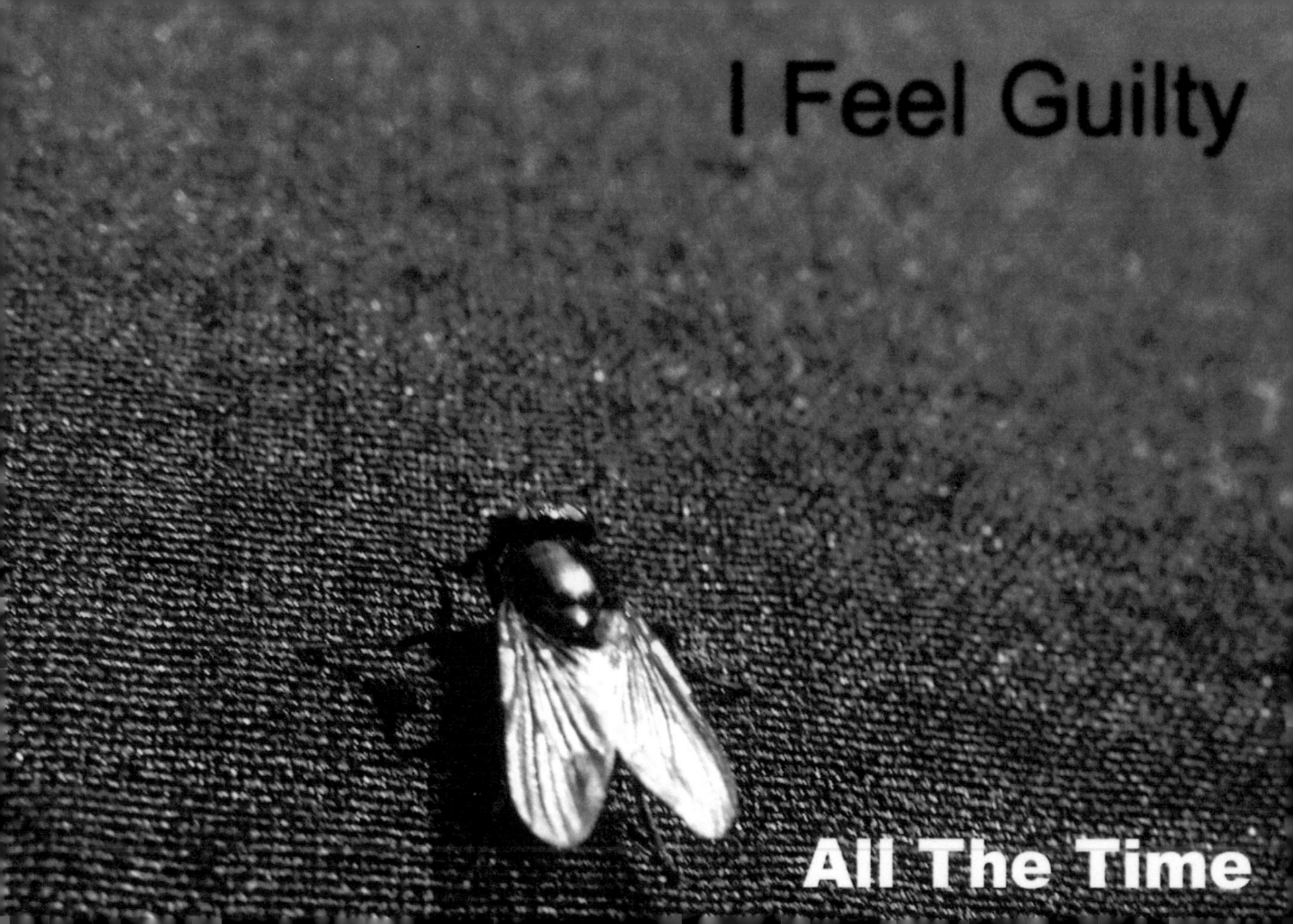
I Feel Guilty
All The Time

I waste
office supplies
because
I hate
my boss.

MESSAGE

Message For

from

number

date

38

I save all the staples I pull out at work.

they're in a box in my desk.

it weighs over a pound and a half.

I USED TO FERTILIZE A RING IN OUR LAWN EVERY TIME I MOWED IT.

IT GREW.

MY PARENTS still think it was ALIENS.

57 + 375 = 432

628 + 56 = 684

I am a successful, college-educated, 50-year-old businesswoman.

I still need to count with my fingers to add.

785.95
+ 128.24
+ 887.67

1801.86

There is a skittle on the bathroom floor at my job. Every time I go pee, I am tempted to eat it.

There is also a chocolate kiss under my desk. Its been there since I started, 1'1/2 years ago. I still might eat it.

Front

... It doesn't
stop Me
from wondering
what they do
see.

Post Secret
13345 Copper
Ridge Road
Germantown, MD
20874-3454

Teddy Bears USA 37

HONOLULU HI 968
PM
5 MAR

GREETINGS FROM
PENDER

Post Secret
13345 Copper Ridge Rd
Germantown, MD
20874-
3454

Back: I married someone I don't love because I wanted to wear the dress.

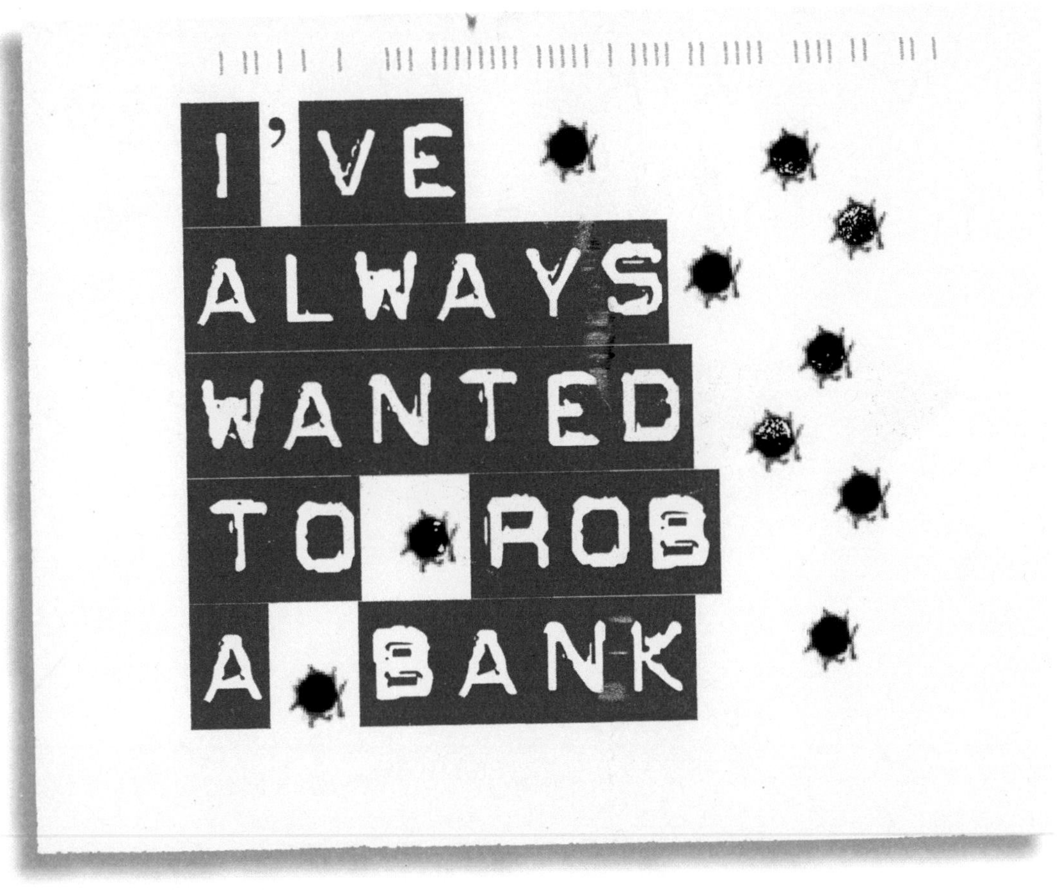
I'VE
ALWAYS
WANTED
TO ROB
A BANK

I DONT LIKE IT WHEN
MY HUSBAND LOOKS INTO MY

WHEN WE HAVE SEX. HE MIGHT
SEE MY SECRET.

.... i want to be kidnapped, stripped naked, then bound in clear wrap to a signpost in the middle of downtown....

.... and no one can set me free....

I ATE ALL THE BLUEBERRIES

(AND THEY WERE DELICIOUS)

There was no deer.

I was just driving too fast.

I can't tell my mom about the rape... She wouldn't want to know. AND IT **KILLS** ME.

I became a COP
so I could try to

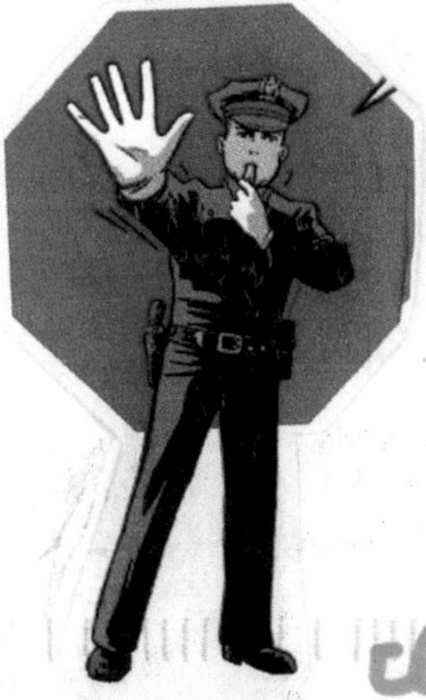

STOP

myself.

It's not working...

I'm happy
and lucky
but I've never
told anyone.

3 years ago, I tried to kill myself...

Now I'm 18 + people say I'm happy...

But I still want to die...

Post 13345

Germantown, MD

USX 20874-3454

Secret Copper Ridge Rd.

20874/3454

58

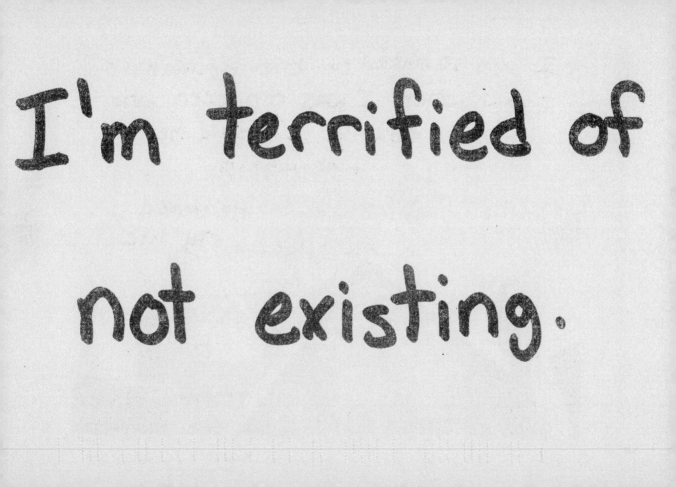

I am so grateful to the psychiatrist I saw when I was nineteen, who told me I would be fine again.

He saved my life.

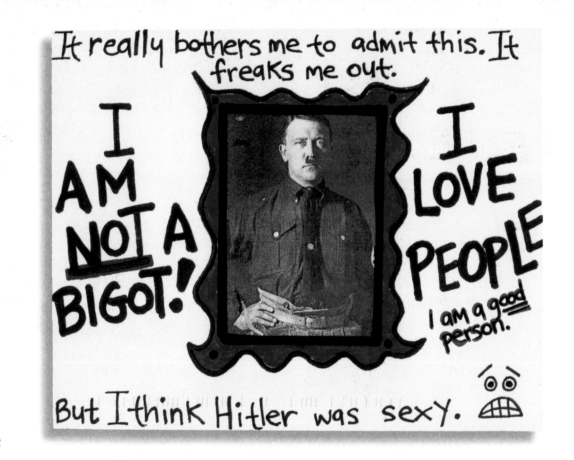

When I was a young teenager I used to babysit my next door neighbours son. When he was asleep I would go into their bedroom and go through their bedside drawers. I found a packet of condoms. I put a pin through the middle of each of them, and thus ensured myself another 5 years of babysitting!

When I'm mad at my husband....

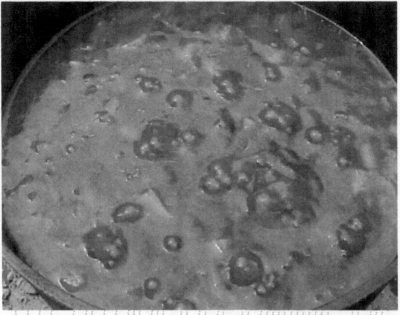

...I put boogers in his soup.

I'm really scared of losing all of my weight because then I will be forced to face my fear of men and have no where to hide

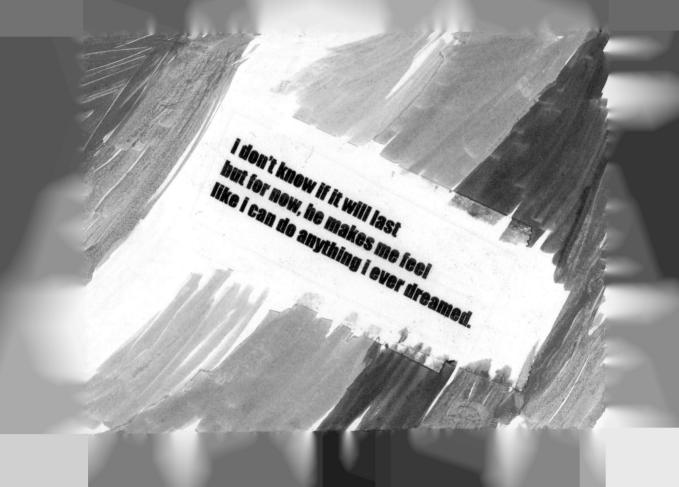

I WILL NEVER STOP LOVING HER

i fear that
i'm going to
be alone for
the rest of
my life.....

and i don't
want to have
to settle
in order
not to be.

68

I get angry

words bad

bad

I when

I

on my toaster strudel.

I HAVE FINALLY SPOKEN MY SECRET
OUT LOUD

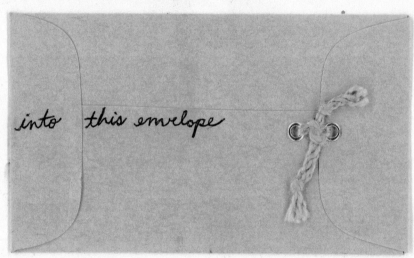

into this envelope

AND SEALED IT FOREVER.

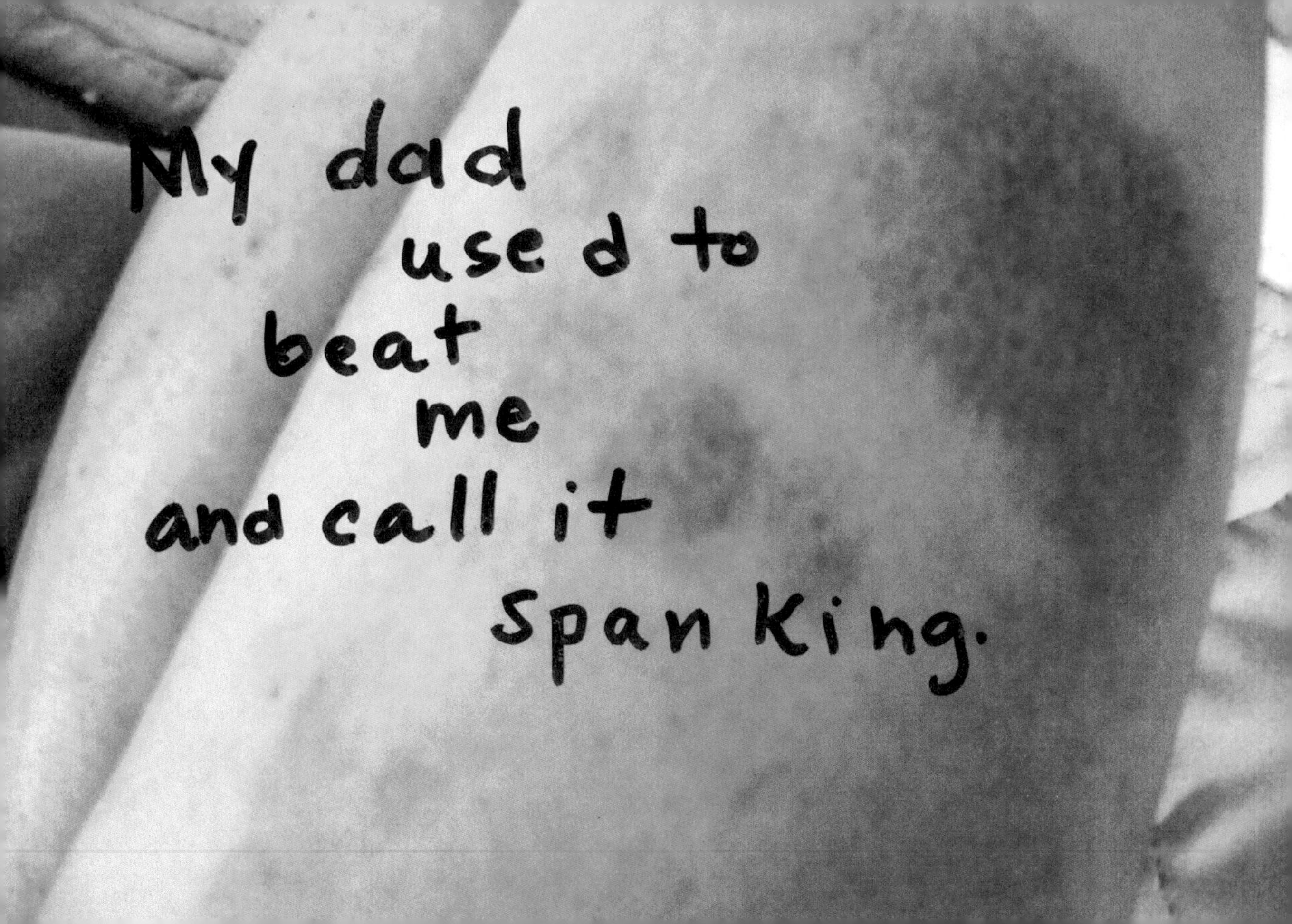
My dad
used to
beat
me
and call it
Spanking.

FOR YEARS

I hurt myself
So that he'd notceme.

Back: I steal small things from my friends to keep memories of how much I love them. 75

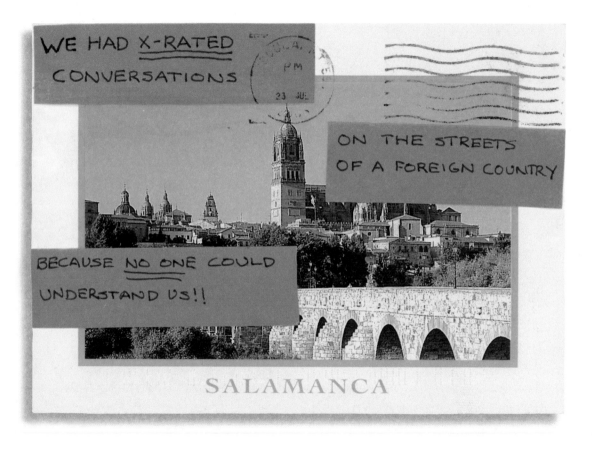

WE HAD X-RATED CONVERSATIONS

ON THE STREETS OF A FOREIGN COUNTRY

BECAUSE NO ONE COULD UNDERSTAND US!!

SALAMANCA

When I was 7 I hid under my parents' BED.

...so I could see what my Dad's penis looked like after his morning shower.

if i had a
million dollars,
i would give
it all away
for one more
day with her
like it used to
be in the
beginning.

FUCK *FUCK* FUCK FUCK FUCK FUCK FUCK

I don't like to use foul language out loud...
Instead, I write it down as many times as I can
on a piece of paper whenever I feel the urge.
After that, I immediately destroy the paper
so no one will find it.

FUCK FUCK FUCK FUCK FUCK FUCK FUCK FUCK FUCK FUCK FUCK FUCK FUCK

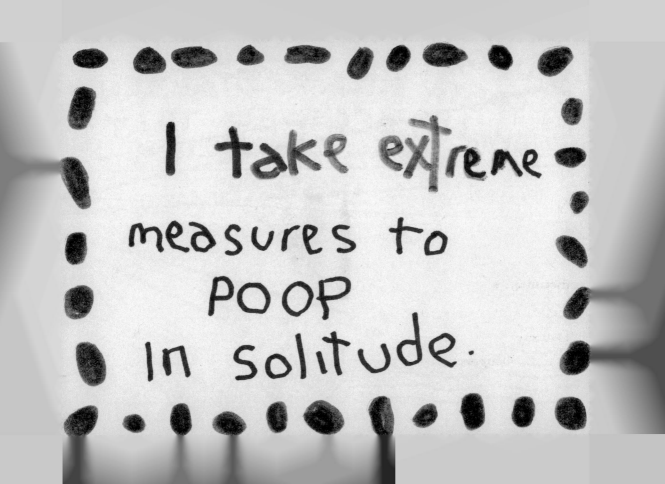

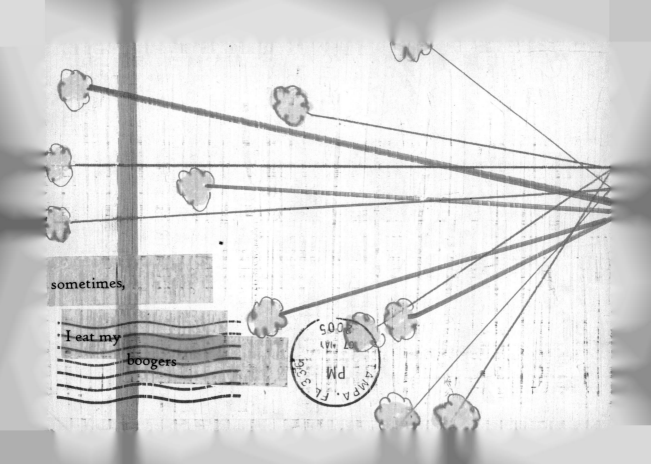

sometimes,

I eat my

boogers

When most people talk to me, I'm thinking, "What an idiot!"
DUMBASS.
UH HUH... OH, YES... I AGREE.
AND WHAT YOU NEED TO BLAH BLAH BLAH LET ME KNOW WHEN YOU BLAH BLAH IF YOU NEED HELP BLAH BLAH WEASELS BLAH BLANCMANGE CHUTNEY DER BLAUE REITER...

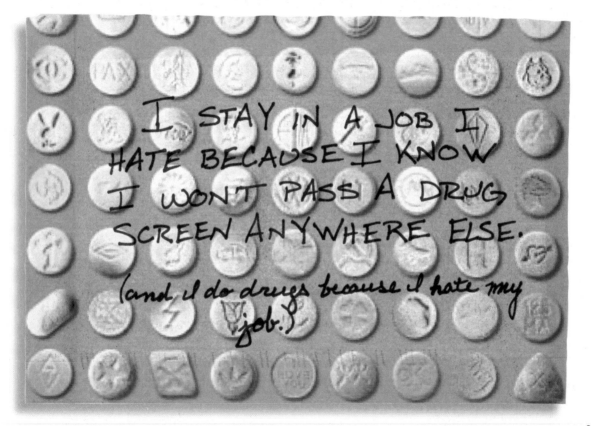

my dad died when i was 9 and i
convinced myself he'd faked his own
death for some reason (undercover
agent, chased by mob, etc.) and that
he'd come back someday.

when i was 12 i found out from my
psychiatrist that this is a pretty
stupid idea

i'm 25 now

i still wonder when it'll be safe
for him to come out of hiding and
find me

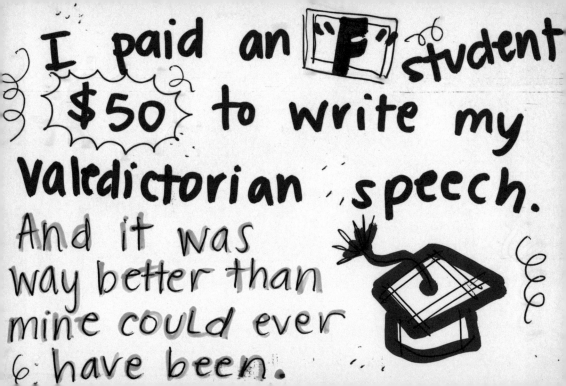

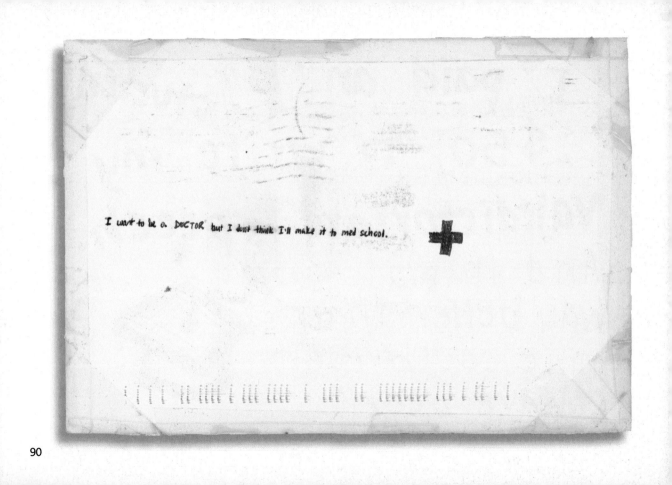

I want to be a DOCTOR but I dont think I'll make it to med school.

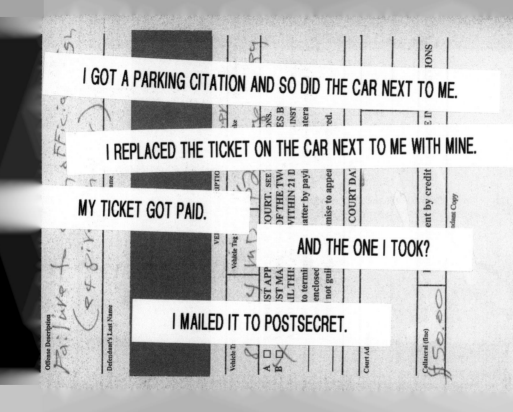

I GOT A PARKING CITATION AND SO DID THE CAR NEXT TO ME.

I REPLACED THE TICKET ON THE CAR NEXT TO ME WITH MINE.

MY TICKET GOT PAID.

AND THE ONE I TOOK?

I MAILED IT TO POSTSECRET.

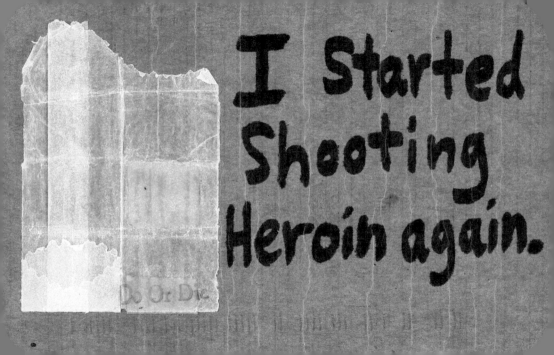

From:

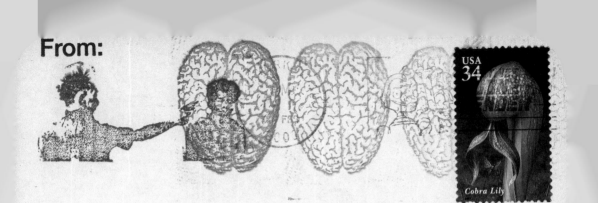

TO: POSTSECRET
13345 COPPER RIDGE ROAD
GERMANTOWN, MD.
20874

Sometimes after dark my friends and I strip down to our bras and panties and run around our local park, swing on the swings and feel so **free**. Afterwards I sketch it.

We call it **Liberation**.

I tell people that I don t believe in God,

when really,

I just refuse to worship a god

that would let my grandfather

HURT me

like he did.

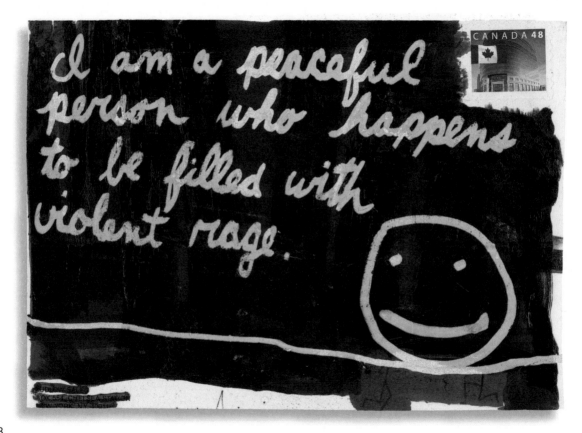

"Sometimes just the act of sharing a painful secret can relieve some of the pain."

—Maryland

I pray for this girl to flunk the ivy league and become a gas attendant

105

	68	Amount paid with request for extension to file (see page 54)	68	
	69	Other payments from: **a** ☐ Form 2439 **b** ☐ Form 4136 **c** ☐ Form 8885	**69**	
	70	Add lines 63, 64, 65a, and 66 through 69. These are your **total payments** . . . . ▶		

Refund

Direct deposit?
See page 54
and fill in 72b,
72c, and 72d.

71	If line 70 is more than line 62, subtract line 62 from line 70. This is the amount you **overpaid**
72a	Amount of line 71 you want **refunded to you** . . . . ▶
▶ b	Routing number	▶ c Type: ☐ Checking ☐ Savings
▶ d	Account number
73	Amount of line 71 you want **applied to your 2005 estimated tax** ▶	**73**

Amount You Owe

74	**Amount you owe.** Subtract line 70 from line 62. For details on how to pay, see page 55 ▶
75	Estimated tax penalty (see page 55)	**75**

Third Party Designee

Do you want to allow another person to discuss this return with the IRS (see page 56)? ☐ **Yes.**

Designee's name ▶   Phone no. ▶ (   )   Personal identific... number (PIN)

Sign Here

Joint return?
See page 17.
Keep a copy
for your
records.

Under penalties of perjury, I declare that I have examined this return and accompanying schedules and statements, an... belief, they are true, correct, and complete. Declaration of preparer (other than taxpayer) is based on all information of w...

▶ Your signature *I. M. A. Crook*   Date   Your occupation

Spouse's signature. If a joint return, **both** must sign.   Date   Spouse's occupation

Paid Preparer's Use Only

Preparer's signature ▶   Date   Check if self-employed ☐

Firm's name (or yours if self-employed), address, and ZIP code ▶   EIN

Phone no.

106

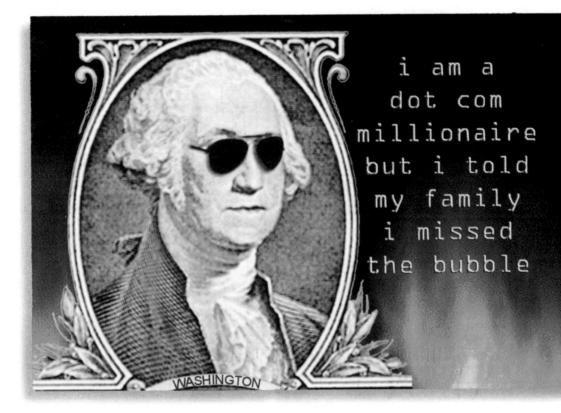

HOW

I've stopped cutting myself but started plucking my pubic hair out with tweezers instead.

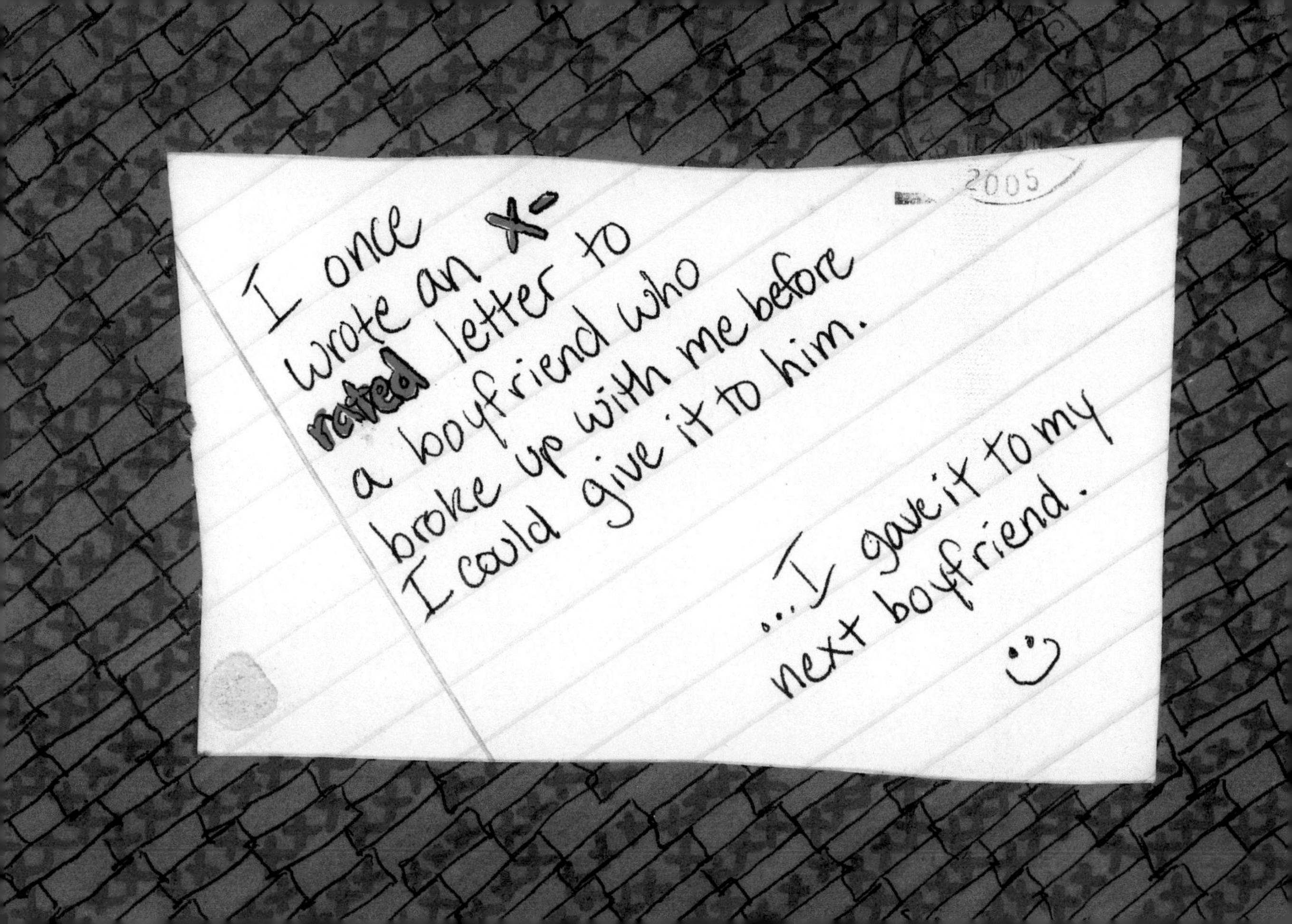

I once
wrote an X-
rated letter to
a boyfriend who
broke up with me before
I could give it to him.

...I gave it to my
next boyfriend.

2005

I believe that my dead grandmother watches me
with great disappointment every time I masturbate.

i considered pressing statutory rape charges.

just so he'd regret breaking my heart.

but ~~then~~ he'd never want me back

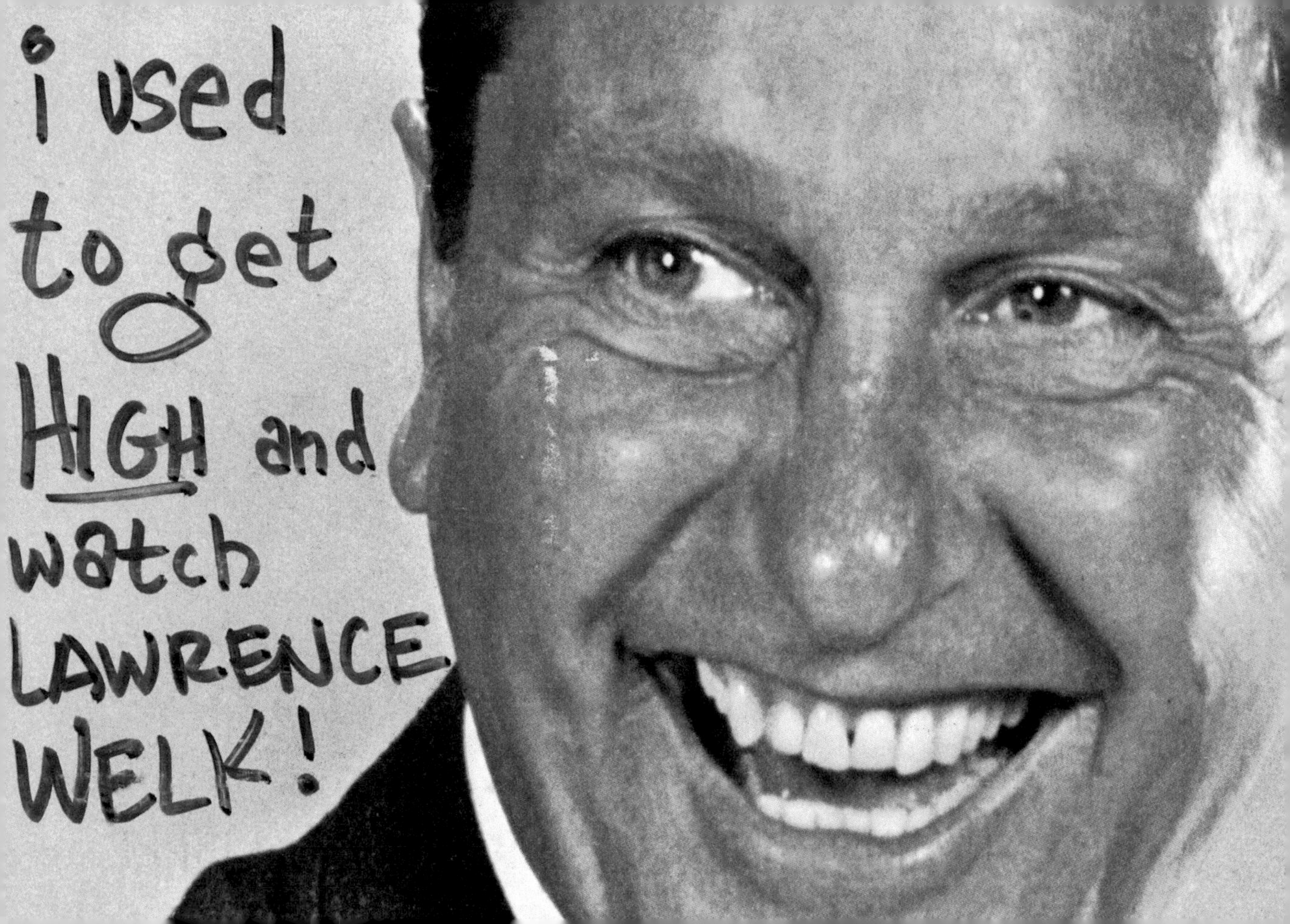
i used to get HIGH and watch LAWRENCE WELK!

I tell everyone I'm **allergic** to cucumbers.

I'm not.

But now I'm scared to eat them.

Because I even told myself.

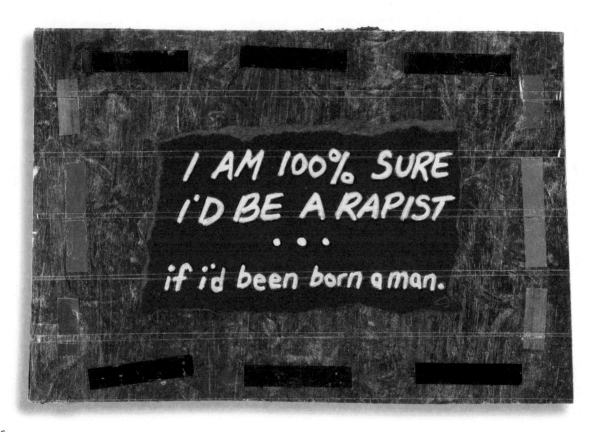

116

Income	**1** Wages, salaries, and tips. This should be shown in box 1 of your Form(s) W-2. Attach your Form(s) W-2.	
Attach Form(s) W-2 here.		**1**
Enclose, but do not attach, any payment.	**2** Taxable interest. If the total is over $1,500, you cannot use Form 1040EZ.	**2**
	3 Unemployment compensation and Alaska Permanent Fund dividends (see page 13).	**3**
	4 Add lines 1, 2, and 3. This is your adjusted gross income.	**4**

Income from teaching creative writing...$32,654.00

d Total number of exemptions claimed.

Income		
Attach Form(s) W-2	**7** Wages, salaries, tips, etc. Attach Form(s) W-2.	**7**

Income from writing creatively...............$0.00

(See Instruction 20).
Print your numbers like this ⋅ 0 1 2 3 4 5 6 7 8 9 ⋅ not like this Ø 4 7

INCOME
1. Adjusted gross income from your federal return (See Instruction 11) .... ▶ | 1 |
1a. Wages, salaries and/or tips (See Instruction 11) .... ▶ | 1a |

ADDITIONS TO INCOME (See Instruction 12)

Doll

I thought I was in love with him

All of my life people
have told me I'm not
special...
I'm very easy to
replace.

After 43 years it
has
finally sunk in.
I finally get it.

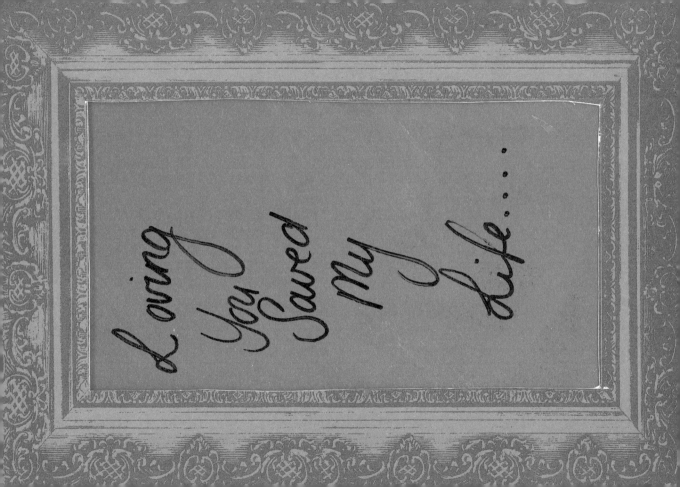

I always wait a few
days before returning e-mails
from my friends because
I don't want them to think
I have nothing better to do

I make up fantasy stories
because my real life SUCKS
And now my fantasy life is starting to SUCK, too.

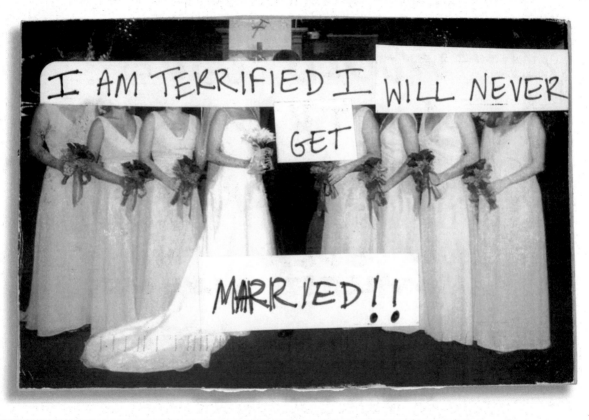

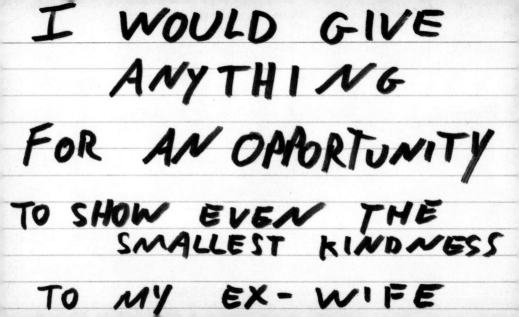

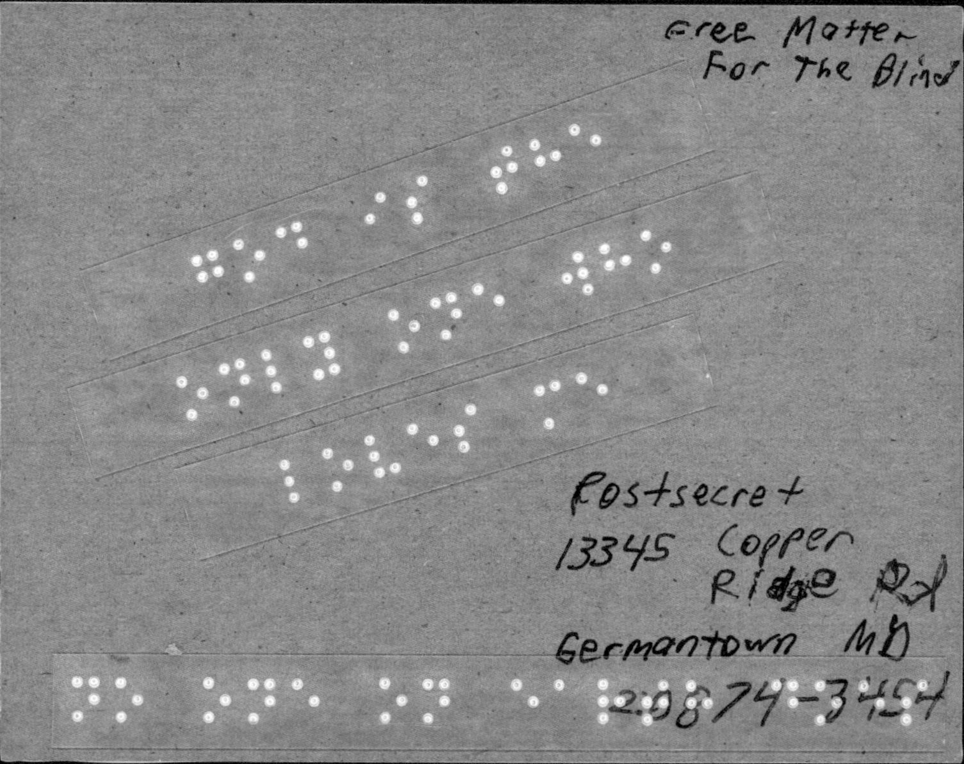

Free Matter
For The Blind

Postsecret
13345 Copper
Ridge Rd
Germantown MD
20874-3454

Braille: god is the only one who loves me
no one else on earth does

The love of my life is ugly.

If I had
to save ONE
person in the
world, I would
ALWAYS choose
← HER.

My dog knew all my secrets, but one.
I put rat poison out back to get rid of a family of rats.
In around five days I had no more rats.
Around two weeks later, I had no dog.
I hope someone can learn from my mistake.
Max, I'm so sorry.
We miss you so, so much.

When people upset me
I draw pictures of them

Cleveland

on Buses going to HELL
Disaster or OHIO

100% PURE

EXTRA VIRGIN...

Front

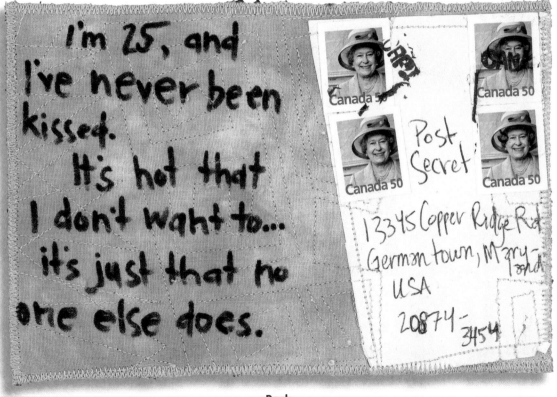

I'm 25, and I've never been kissed. It's hot that I don't want to... it's just that no one else does.

Post Secret

13345 Copper Ridge Rd
Germantown, Maryland
USA
20874-3454

Canada 50
Canada 50
Canada 50
Canada 50

Front

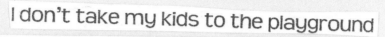

I don't take my kids to the playground

because I don't like talking to the other moms.

HE WASN'T CHEATING ON YOU.

123 · Learn to listen. Opportunity sometimes knocks very softly.

BUT SINCE YOU CHOSE TO BLAME ME ANYWAY... HE WILL BE.

i wish my parents said i LOVE YOU...
I can't remember hearing them say it...
EVER!

I LOVE BLACK GIRLS

AND I AM WHITE

(IT's OK!)

"Dear Frank,
How I wish I could hug everyone and tell them that it's ok. It's ok to be scared and angry and hurt and selfish. It's part of being human."

—Ohio

When my friends go on diets,

I discourage them.

This is because I

really just want them to be

fatter

than me.

I can eat a dozen DONUTS in one sitting

I dreamt I was allergic to make-up.

Now I am.

151

There is reason to believe
I was a pre-honeymoon baby ...

it's a Problem girl!

... and evidence
that my mother still has not
forgiven me for this.

My SISTER and I EXPLORED EACH other sexually as CHILDREN. As the OLDER girl I feel GUILTY that I may have MOLESTED her.

Honestly, I'm glad your
Uncle died, because he
molested me that time in
the 7th grade that I spent
the night at your house...
He told me that I liked it. I hope
he likes it in his grave...

WHEN I WAS 7, the neighborhood bully stopped ①
me on my bike and told me that if I didn't let
him touch my butt that he would hurt me and
my 5 year old sister. Terrified, I let him. The
next day at school, I was at a water
fountain when he came up w/ a
group of boys. He told them what
he had done to me.
Ashamed, all I
could do, was
drink from the
fountain and not
look up until they went away. To this day,
when I feel shame - I get thirsty.

To:
POSTSECRET
13345 Copper Ridge
Road
Germantown, MD
20874 - 3454

20874/3454

158

I believe that one day I will like myself.

PostSecret
13345 Copper Ridge Rd
Germantown, MD
20874-3454

When I was 3 my dad liked me to brush his thick red hair. One day he asked and I said I didn't want to. I never saw him again.- he went away and then he died..

I am 65 & some days I still think it was my fault.

163

I feel guilty about sometimes wishing that I didn't have children.
I don't dare say it out loud for fear I might trigger something bad happening to them.

bad mother

My parents think I'm
checking my e-mail
when I'm reading
online erotica.

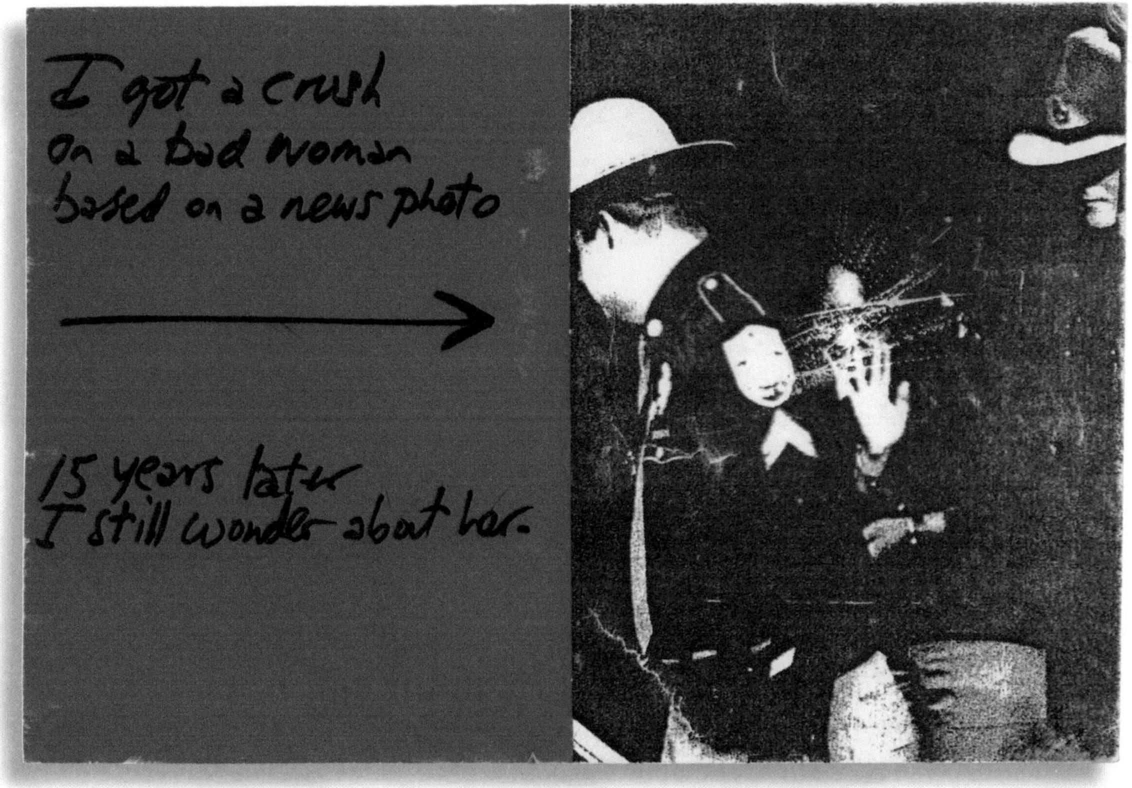
I got a crush
on a bad woman
based on a news photo
15 years later
I still wonder about her.

I love getting my period...

It gives me an excuse
to be bitchy and irritable
and to take naps.

Sometimes I cancel all of my
appointments in a day. Tell
everyone I'm sick... and
pleasure myself all day.
I have so much
fun—I'm exhausted—
almost paralysed
by pleasure.
        The next day...
I go back to work.

Back: When I was 12 my Mom joined the crowd of relatives who were laughing at me cause I couldn't carry a tune. I never whistled again.

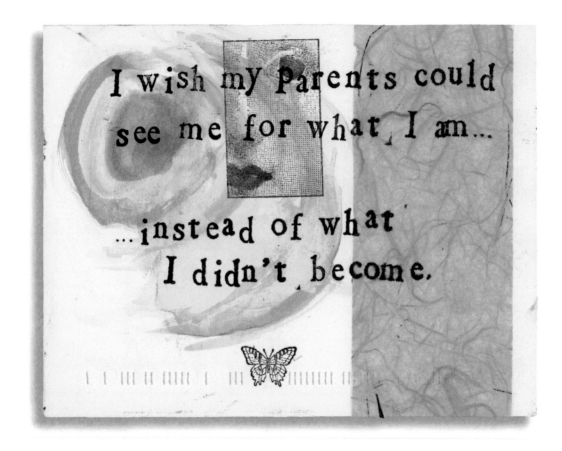

I wish my Parents could see me for what I am...

...instead of what I didn't become.

My Math Teacher
and my parents
told me - they (4, 0)
4 = x
were proud of me.

I believed
my teacher.

#20

×50/50

Excellent!

x-4 = 2x-8

3x = x+4
- y -x
2x = 4
x = 2

= 169   y² + 8y + 104 = 169

(2, 7)

(0, -13)

I love one
of my children.

178

everytime i approach an overpass,
i think how easy it would be to simply
turn the wheel ever so slightly to the
left and find peace, at long last...

I play a game when I'm in church.

For every person who passes by me

to go up to receive communion

I think to myself:

"How much money would someone have to pay me to have sex with them?"

I miss feeling
close to God.

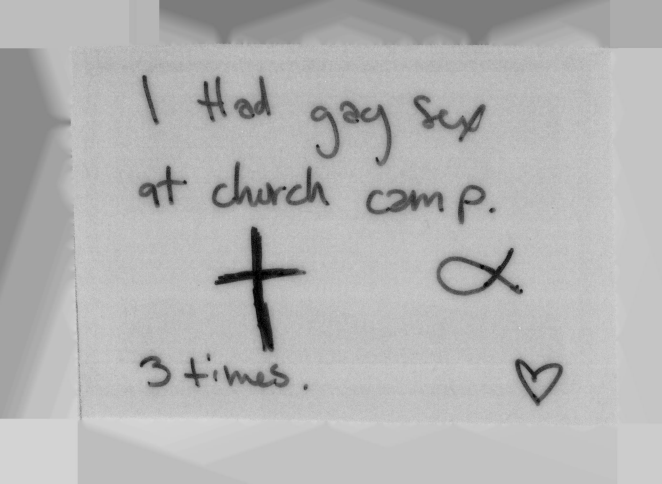

what hurts more than losing you...

is knowing you're not fighting to keep me.

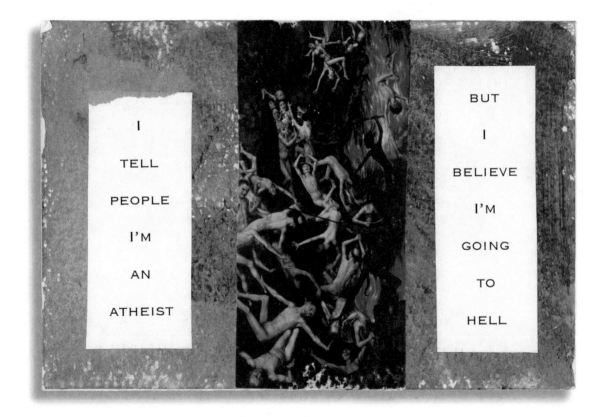

I TELL PEOPLE I'M AN ATHEIST

BUT I BELIEVE I'M GOING TO HELL

when i see an ugly bride,
what i am really seeing is

a glimmer
of hope
for the
future

[maybe i will marry, someday.]

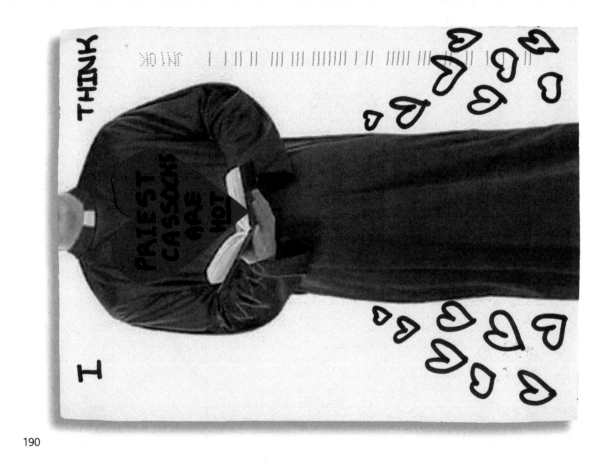

190

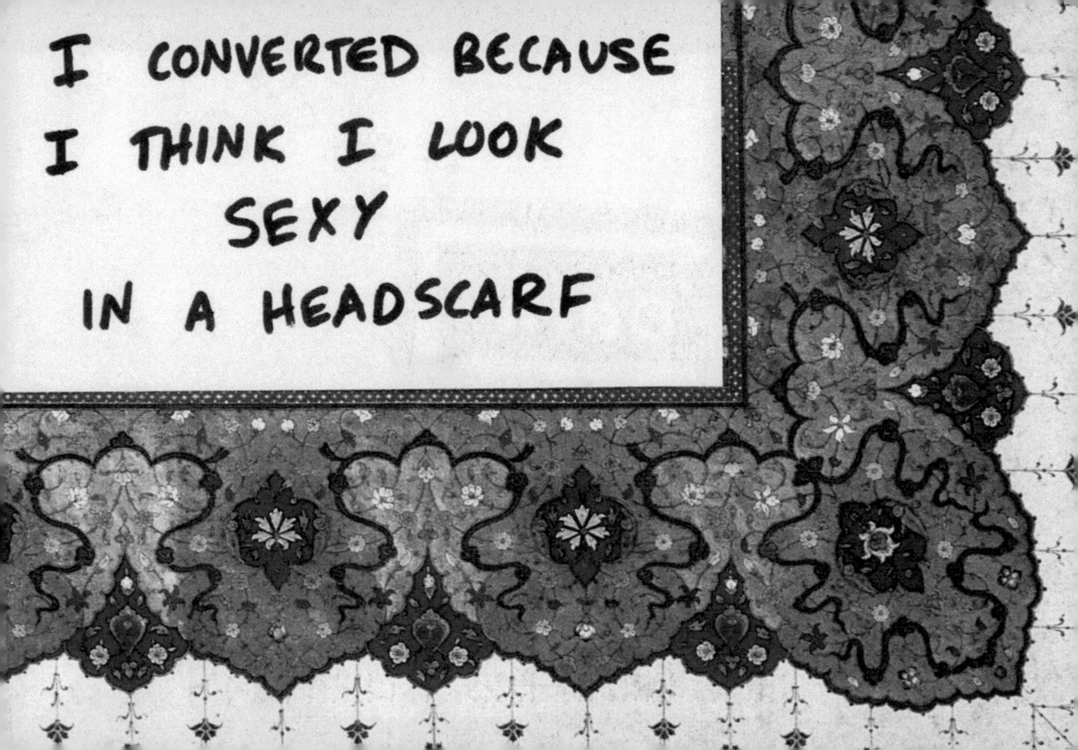

I CONVERTED BECAUSE
I THINK I LOOK
SEXY
IN A HEADSCARF

My friends and family think I am this sweet innocent girl. But, they don't know I've posted nude photo's of myself on the internet!

i show pictures of my feet to a man online so he'll buy me stuff.

I DREAM: There is a Lover who will know that I'm faking.

さいはての海に浮かぶ 漁場の標識 帆揚瀬 tou

"Dear Frank,
So many of my secrets are
there, without even sending
a card."

—Mexico

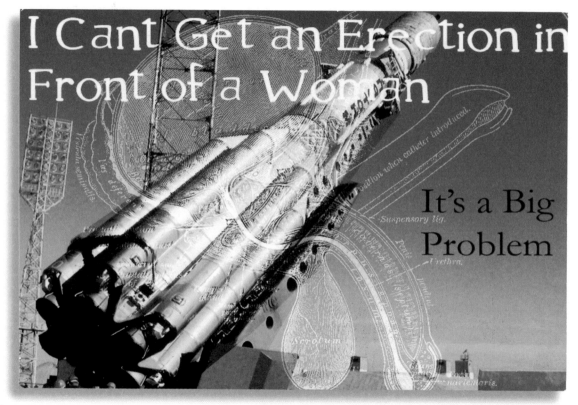

202

i pulled a muscle in my neck while masturbating !!!

i couldn't move my head for 3 days.

(i told my husband it was from moving furniture)

203

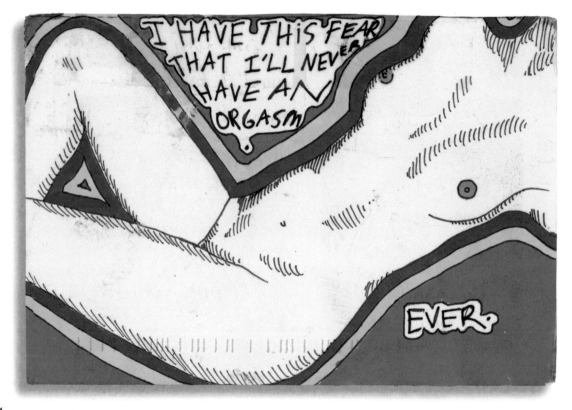

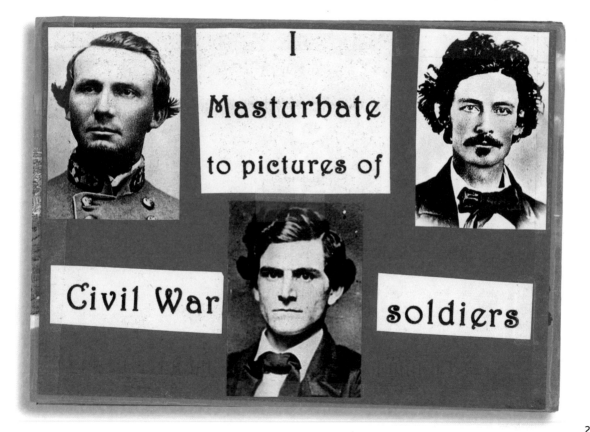

I FEEL REALLY BAD WHEN I HAVE SEXUAL FANTASIES ABOUT THE DEAD.

1943-2001

Shhh!
My Grandma
THINKS I'M
CHRISTIAN
BUT i've been writing Books
about being an Atheist!

i

checked

into

a hotel

next to the

train tracks of a

busy Long Island

commuter train line

into new york city . . .

& exhibited myself

nude at night

in the window

when trains passed

I loved it.

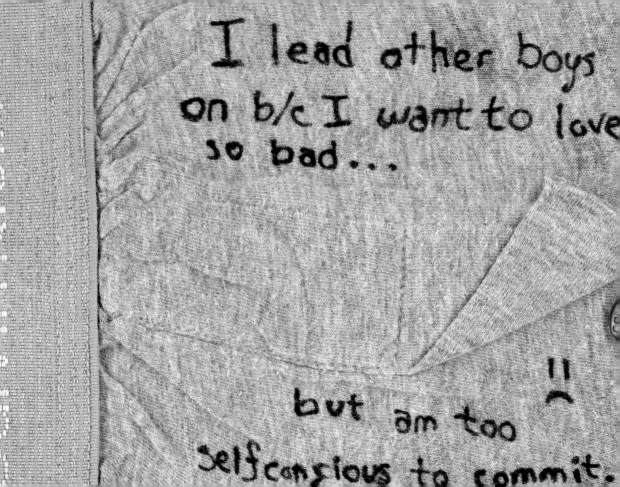

211

SOMETIMES I WISH I WAS

A BOY⚲

SO I COULD MAKE OUT WITH GIRLS.

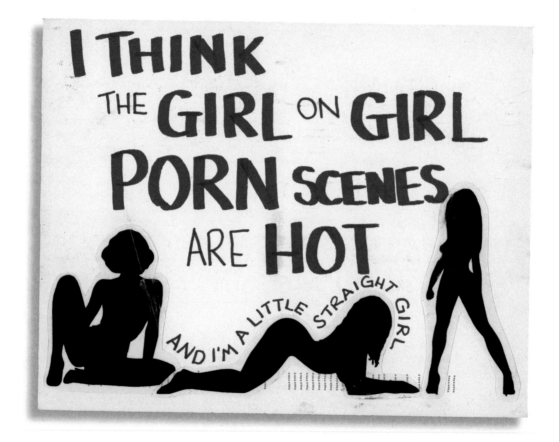

213

214

215

SOMETIMES, I HOPE THE DRUGS WILL TAKE ME AWAY BEFORE THE LONLINESS EVER GETS ITS CHANCE.

I think
that ads
for lingere
are sexier
than porn.
magazines,
and cheaper.

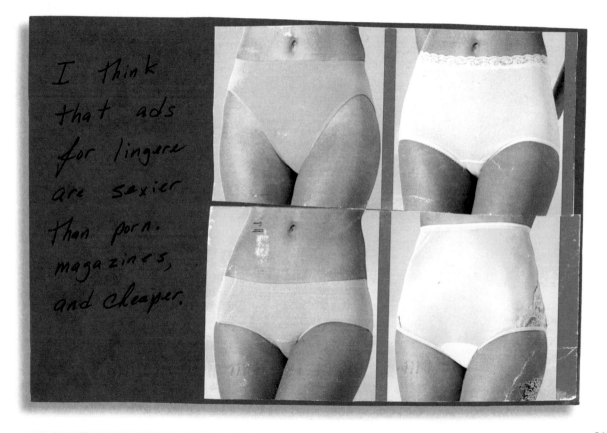

I've created over a dozen tee-shirts with quotes and photos from obscure films in hopes that someone will recognize them

and be the

true-blue best friend that I've always dreamed of.

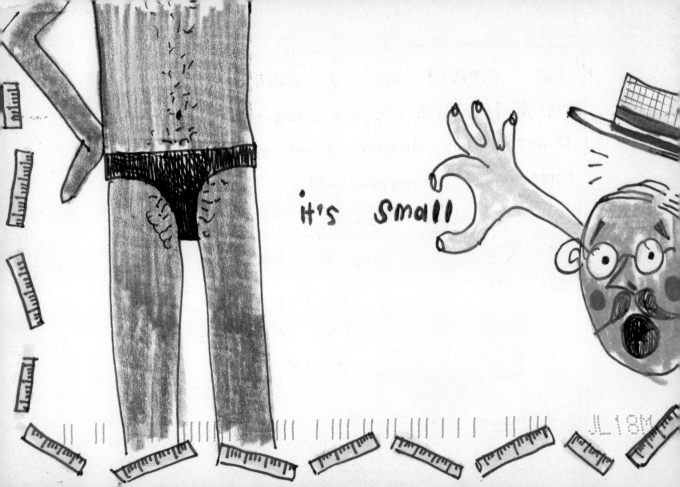

I am in therapy.
Learning to
Love my self
For the First
in my
Life   I am 26.

My neighbor was making too much noise. So I cranked up the volume on the stereo. He came over and gave my teenage son shit. I just stood there and never stood up for my son. I love my son. I'm sorry I did this. I can't stop my tears as I write this. I'm 60 yrs old and will never forgive myself. I have never talked to my son about this

My father was jailed for the rape and molestation of his girlfriend's daughters. He's been there several years. I've always suspected he molested me, as well. But I've never said anything, and I'm scared to find out if my suspicions are true. I'm not sure if my father is the imprisoned one, or if the one imprisoned is ME.

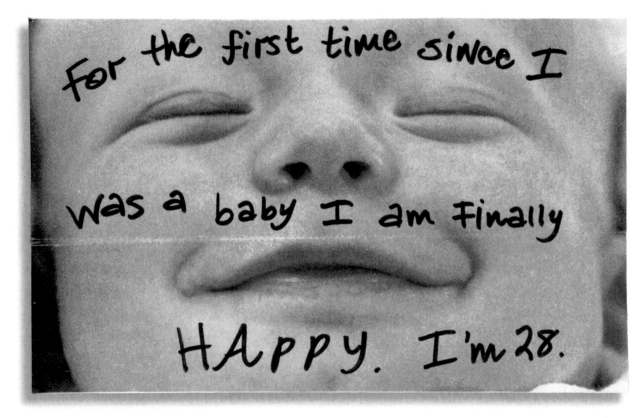

i still beliEVE MY childhood bear is real.

I am in college.

I still talk to her.....

when no one is in the room.

225

I haven't spoken
to my dad in
10 years...
and it kills me everyday.

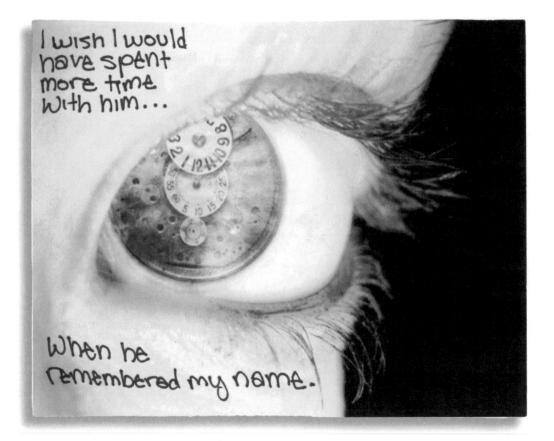

she never gave me a chance

In a CROWD, (Friends, Family, strangers) I always wonder which of us will die FIRST.

Post Secret
13345 Copper Ridge Rd
Germantown, Maryland
USA 20874-3454

HONG KONG
21.04.05
AMC1

HONG KONG, CHINA
中國香港 $3

20874/3993

On back of card: Our one and only photo is hidden behind this postcard . . .
I love you, I miss you, I want you, I need you, but I couldn't tell.

When I find a picture on the ground, or at school, I put them in my scrap book and write a paragraph and pretend the people in it are my friends.

And I dont feel so ALONE

POSTSECRET
13345 COPPER RIDGE
GERMANTOWN, MD
20874-3454

I MAKE EVERYONE
BELIEVE THAT I
LIKE TO BE

Different,

BUT REALLY I JUST
DON'T KNOW HOW
TO FIT IN.

I WISH I WERE A POPULAR IDIOT
INSTEAD OF A LONELY GENIUS.

$$\int_{-\infty}^{\infty} e^{-st} f(t) u(t) \, dt < \heartsuit$$

three years ago my dad died.
one year ago i lost my virginity
to a guy i dated for a month.
if my dad was still alive that
wouldn't have happened.

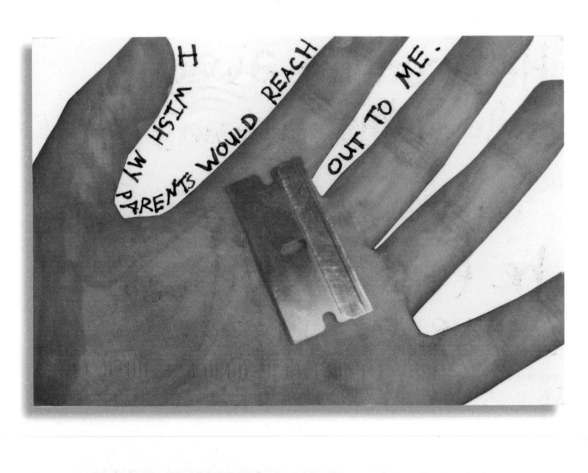

He's running away to follow his dreams...

...part of me is wishing he fails so we can live out mine...

It hurts so much

241

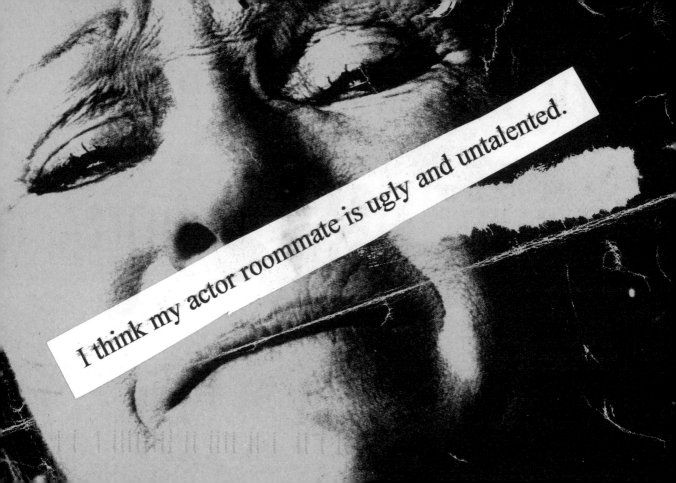

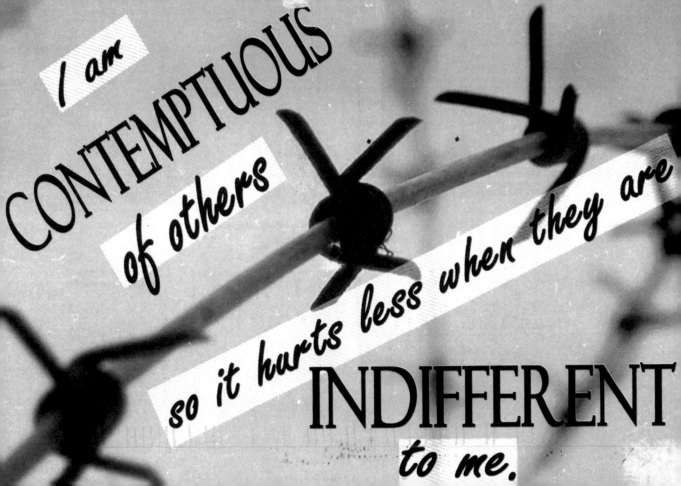

I am CONTEMPTUOUS of others so it hurts less when they are INDIFFERENT to me.

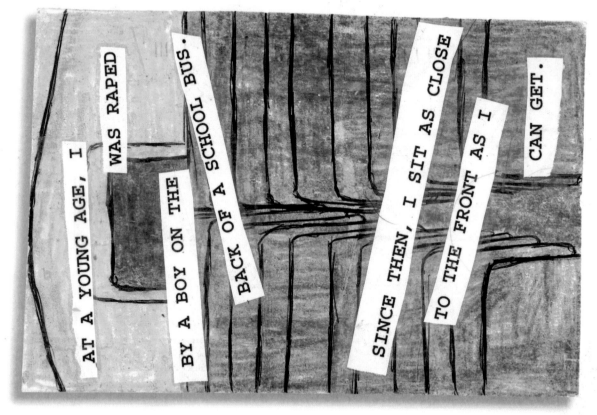

AT A YOUNG AGE, I WAS RAPED BY A BOY ON THE BACK OF A SCHOOL BUS. SINCE THEN, I SIT AS CLOSE TO THE FRONT AS I CAN GET.

HELLO
my name is

I force new acquaintances to address me by my shortened name because it makes me forget my past.

Dear Frank,

"After I created my postcard, I didn't want to be the person with that secret any longer. I ripped up my postcard and I decided to start making changes in my life."

—Texas

I BROKE UP WITH MY BOYFRIEND WHO USED TO CALL ME <u>DARLING</u> WHEN WE <u>MADE LOVE</u> BECAUSE I FELL IN LOVE WITH A MAN WHO CALLS ME <u>SLUT</u> WHEN HE <u>FUCKS</u> ME.

Nothing rhymes with *works*

T TELUS
mobility

2021

VIACOM

Back: I hate billboards so much I have started to vandalise them.

251

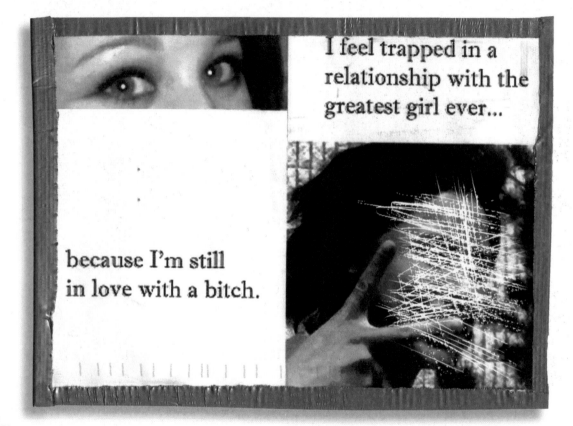

I feel trapped in a relationship with the greatest girl ever...

because I'm still in love with a bitch.

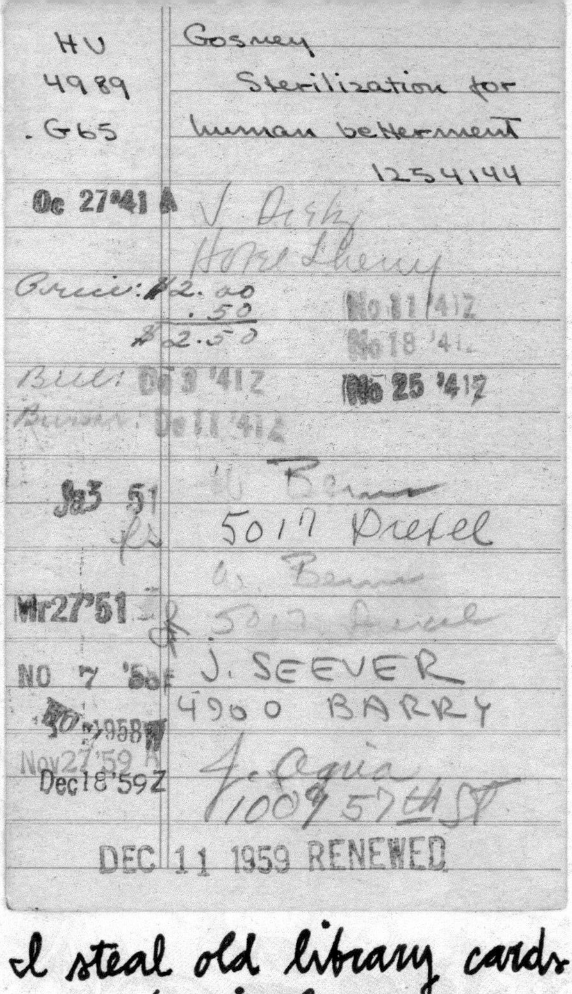

HU
4989
.G65

Gosney
Sterilization for
human betterment
1254144

I steal old library cards.
obscurely—

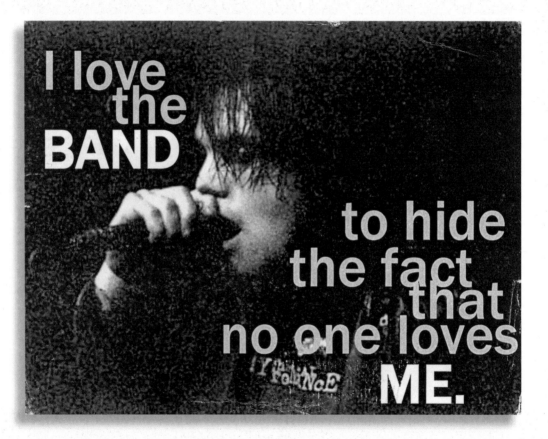

Everyday I type you little
Text messages. I tell you
I love you. I miss you.
Have a wonderful day.
Please be careful.

But I don't send them.
I know I'm not supposed to.

But I hope that somehow,
You know...

I MISS YOU...
I WISH YOU
WOULD CALL...

I am unable to share my secret,
but know this;
The most expensive drink you will ever taste is

free alcohol.

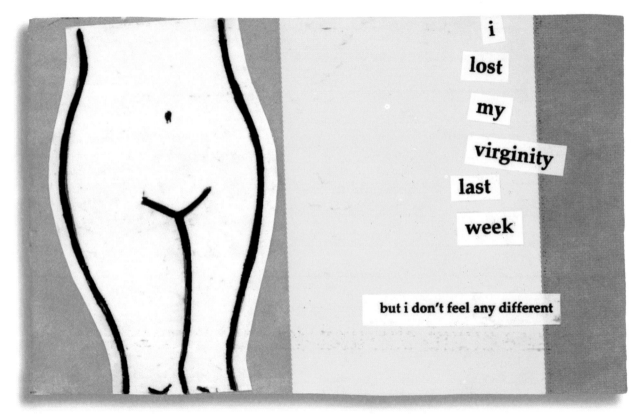

i
lost
my
virginity
last
week

but i don't feel any different

258

I JOINED BECAUSE I WAS PATRIOTIC.

BUT SINCE THEY SUCCEEDED IN CONVINCING ME

MY LIFE IS WORTHLESS, I'M JUST HOPING I

GET SHOT,

RTGOIAUGROIJFDLKANADLKGFNALKTRJLEKRTJLAKJETPAL
DKGFJAKEWRNRNADFDDLKJADGFIEORJYGOIAHGLKADNFG
OIUJTAOIREUJTOAIEJGADGADKNGFADLKGFFDLKJAGFDLKC
LKIJFDGOIUAHARETOIUHERTOIAHEGTOIEHRTOIHAETROIH
IZBVIMDALKGJFLKGLAKDJGFKJFGAOIEWUJRTOIOIQOIWRQ
IETRNEVERWOIEPPALKGCPCPCPCIJHAETKJEWJAIEJREYTIU
ERKJANKGFLIKEDJDAOIJRETPIAJETRLIHADLGUHLGAIUHGFI
ATGIUHATRPUAYOURPIUHANMNZVCKJHADSOGFUREWPTIU
ASMADSM,NFADUHPOETRY.EWOUTROIHWLIJKALJKZLJKHL
AKJNDSKJNDGFAFDLJHGFDPIUEHRTPIUEIUHALUJHEIUHRET
DFLJGKJNAMNZVCMNCBMNADOIHAGLKJHERTIUHATREIUH
RUTUAUAYDIFUAHGDYADSFLKJHAGYALKJHGAYALKHGYA
SDFHJLADSFHLKJQEUTRIPOQUTREIPQETRUIPOQTREUQKL
HGLKJADJKNMZNVCMNZXCMVNXMVCNOIUJADKJHGFDKJH
GFJHADJGHEIRUHTAEOIUTRHANM,ZNCVMNCXZVNMBCXV
LKJHADGFLKJHDLKJGHNDFAKNAMNZCXVMNARDSKIHHFG
IOUAHDTLKJREHLKJAMNZVCXKJHADLKJFHAGFDJHFDGIUE
FGJHADGFIUEHRTGIUANMZNADKGALJHADKJHDGFIUHOER
LUIHARIUHGEAKJNHADJNVNCMXZLHUALUAHRDGIUHALD
FHDFLKJGHADLKJGHAEOIUYEATRKJHALKJHHGFSRYUYFGR
TDTDYTYTHYASDFGHWERTYOIYHFVDECGBJHGYTFKYUU
ILKJAHGIUAHENFGJANHGFDIUAHETRJNBADFJGHADKJGFH
UUAUBSWUEHGTRKIAREKJAHDGNDXHXIARGAUNSIAUHTE
VKJHDSAIUHWEURHATIUYHTIUIUHGAHWQWEIUQWEQKJH
ZXHZIUHSEIUHSDFIUHEIKUGTEIUREDPLDFOKDSGMABNA
EJHRGOIHAGOIHADGOIHREOITHTEOIHAKDKJNZMNZXCM,V
KHAJHAKZXCBIUHESIUHWETIUYWIQIUQIUEWHRATOUHAR
JAGJHAMNBZCOIUHUJGUYUGIOAKUGKIUYGUYTFTRDWERT
TYUJ8JTHGFYYRRRYGNIMKMOOKLOKOJIJINUBUBUYBYVY
FTVYBBKBJHGFTFYTRDFHNVJBHGKNBHKJBHKVJGFCFCDK
LJKBKJBHUYVYTKJVKLOLKLKUYKIUYTFYTFDRDRTDKVFG
GYTTRDCKIYTFGKHGBYTKUHKUKUYFKFRTDJHGDSKHGSI
ADGFLIJADKLJGADKJFGAOIUWRETIOUATREKJMNZCXVMN
GFDIUHERTIUHRETKJHDGJHDGIULALJHBCCXZXCVZVCXZX
XIUHDSFIGUHAPOAUHILRGALUIHDFLGIUHADIUFHADIGUH

I DIDN'T TELL PEOPLE I WAS RUNNING A MARATHON FOR FEAR THEY'D BE NAUSEATED BY VISIONS OF MY FAT ASS BOUNCING DOWN THE STREET.

when i eat, i feel
like a failure.

French: I hate every part of my body (except my hands).

State Capitol, Lansing, Mich.

I only pick up my dog's turds when people are watching

OC-H1003

266

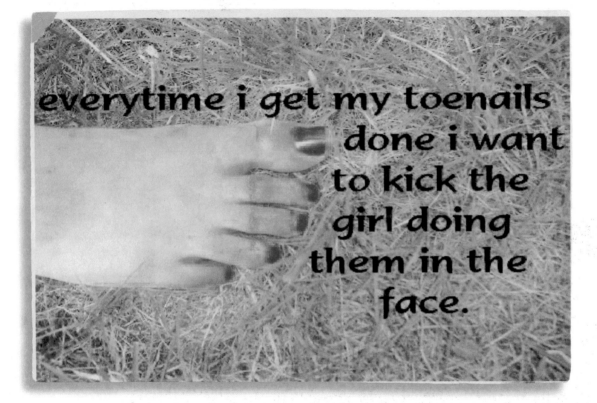

everytime i get my toenails done i want to kick the girl doing them in the face.

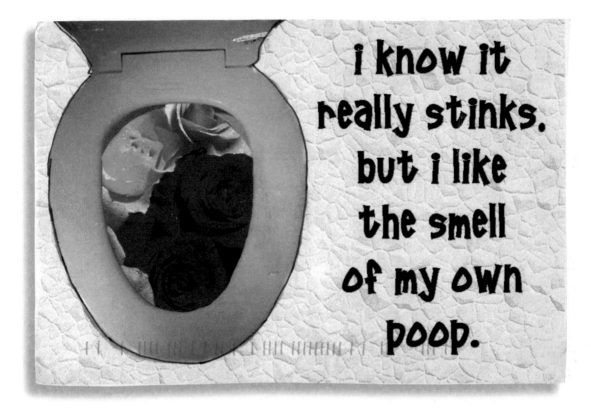

i know it really stinks. but i like the smell of my own poop.

270

Sometimes I romanticize my roots (more "ethnic," more blue collar ....) to be more interesting at chic cocktail parties.
I'm a good liar.

I still haven't told my father that I have the same disease that killed my mother.

violence • black • blue • rape • hit • scream • silence •

LOVE. JOY.

COMPASSION. TRUST.

hope • purple • Sodium • pain • guilt • hate

tears • joy •

I LOVE MY HUSBAND because he's the only MAN I've been with who hasn't hurt my body with violence

AND HE NEVER WILL AND HE NEVER WILL AND HE NEVER WILL AND HE NEVER WILL

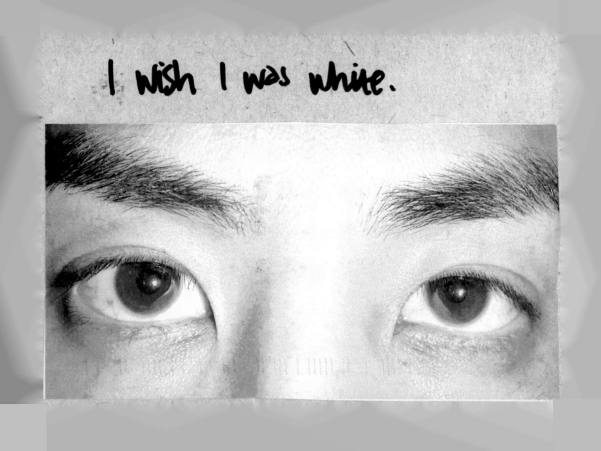

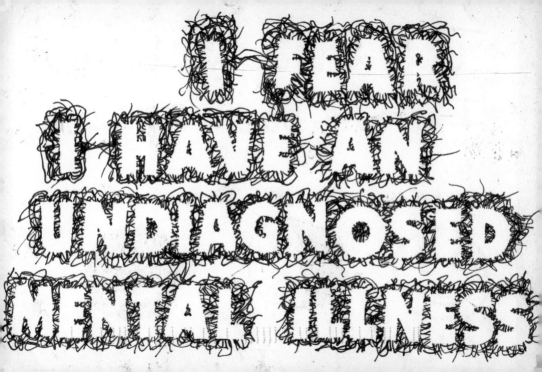

I feel ugly because
I'm half-black, half-white.

I wanted the plane to crash so I wouldn't have to miss him anymore.

I wish I could just walk away

My hands
shake as I
mail this.

(I was so _wrong_.)

postsecret
13345 copper ridge
Rd
Germantown, Maryland
20874-3454

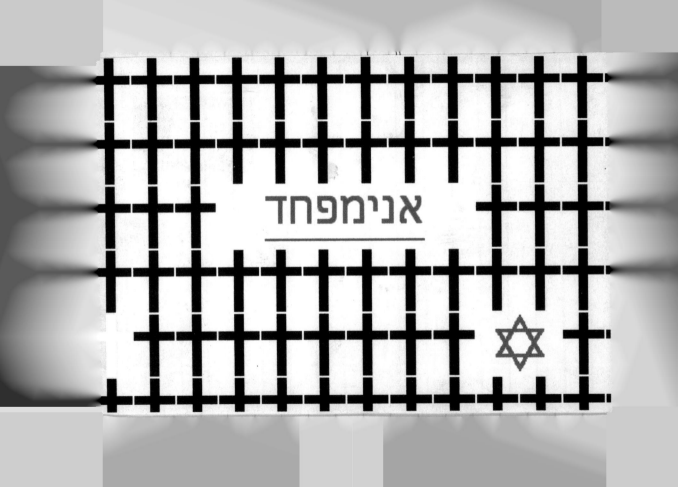

287

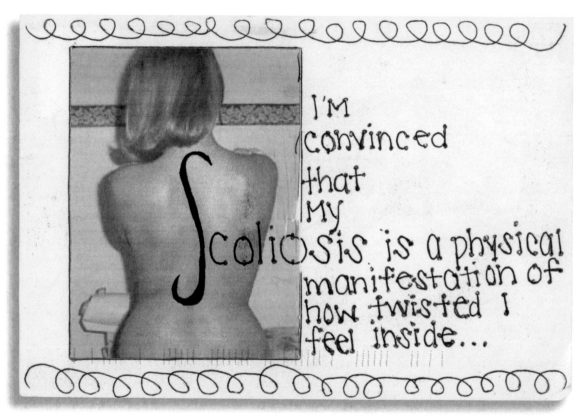

I'M convinced that MY Scoliosis is a physical manifestation of how twisted I feel inside...

289

she isn't yours

my mother took her secret to her grave

Sometimes I think my fiancé isn't THE ONE

Most people believe
that I should hate him
most for hurting me.

But I don't.

I hate him most
for making me think
I deserved it.

I hope he burns in
HELL.

293

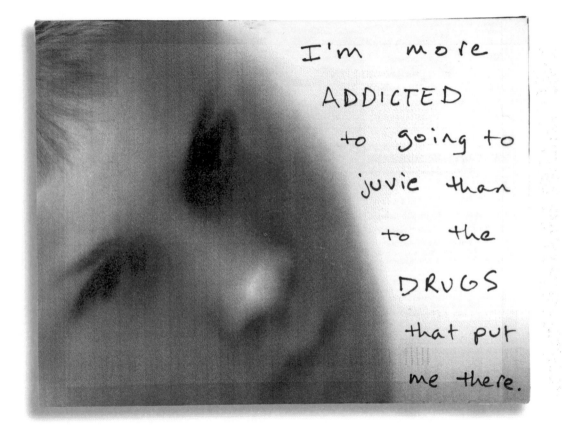

I'm more ADDICTED to going to juvie than to the DRUGS that put me there.

294

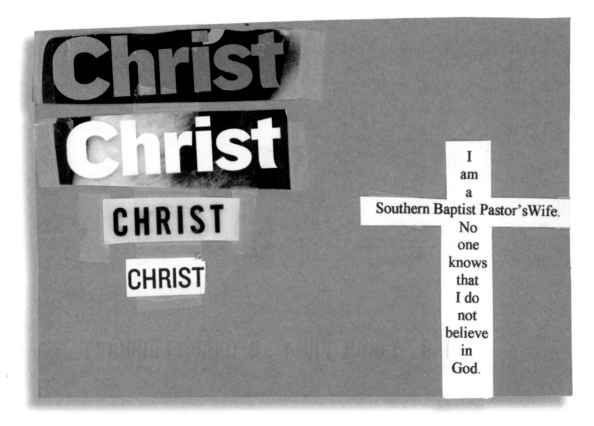

I was seven years old the first time I attempted SUICIDE

thank you

I write the same
thing on all of my

thank you notes, and
I worry that my
relatives will compare them
and find out.

i was probably the only one who
knew he was an addict.

i never said anything.

he died six months ago today.

... I want to die ......

.... a hero

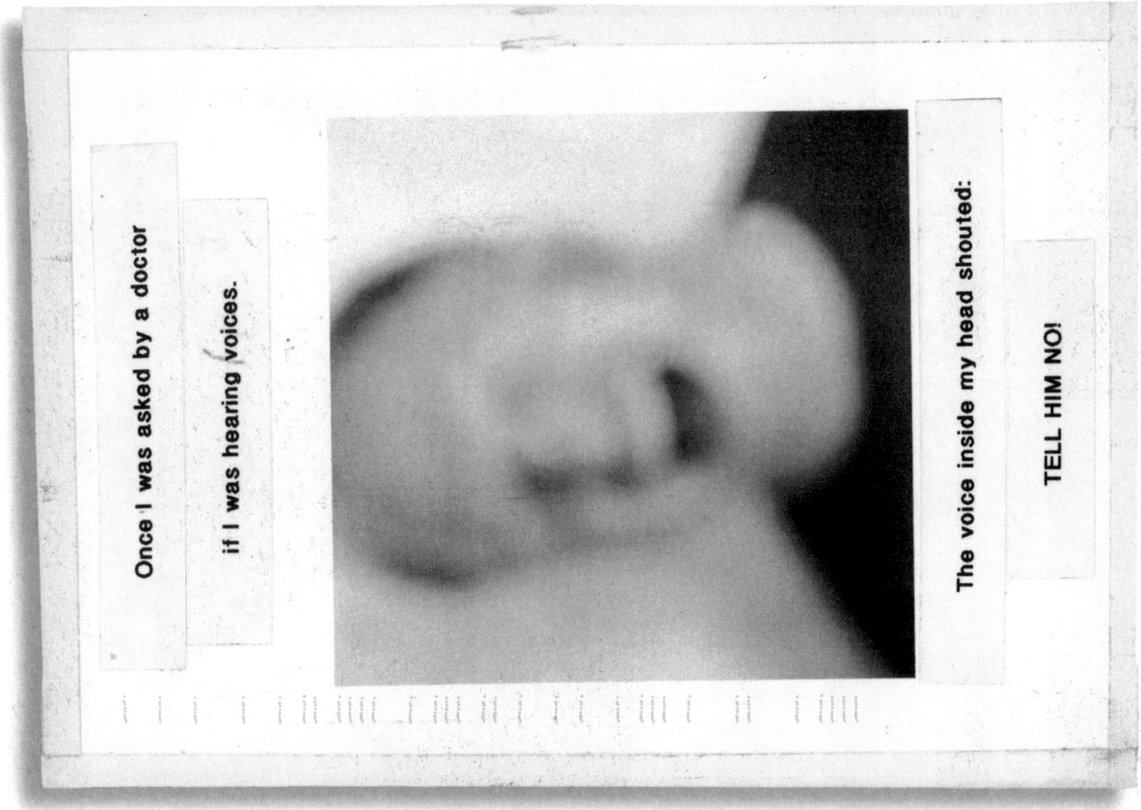

Once I was asked by a doctor

if I was hearing voices.

The voice inside my head shouted:

TELL HIM NO!

303

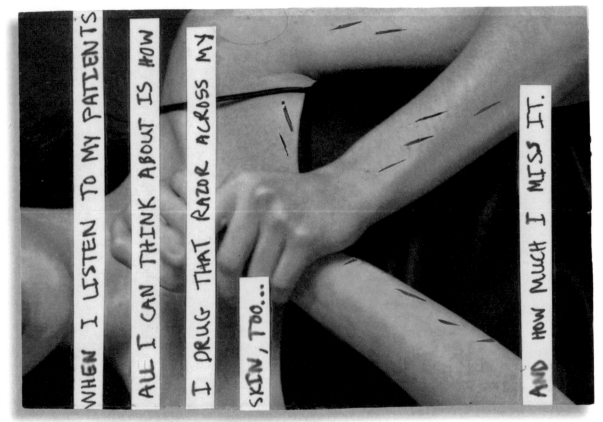

WHEN I LISTEN TO MY PATIENTS

ALL I CAN THINK ABOUT IS HOW

I DRUG THAT RAZOR ACROSS MY

SKIN, TOO...

AND HOW MUCH I MISS IT.

TERN UNION
TELEGRAM
W. P. MARSHALL, PRESIDENT

1213 (7-58)

INTERNATIONAL SERVICE
Check the class of service desired;
otherwise the message will be
sent at the full rate.

FULL RATE	
LETTER TELEGRAM	
SHORE-SHIP	

CHARGE TO THE ACCOUNT OF

TIME FILED

are hereby agreed to

Destination

I ONCE PLANNED 19

TO KILL MY

MOTHER

Senders's name and address (For reference)

Sender's telephone number

This Jackass at my school died. I'm ~~se~~ kind of happy that I don't have to see him any-more.

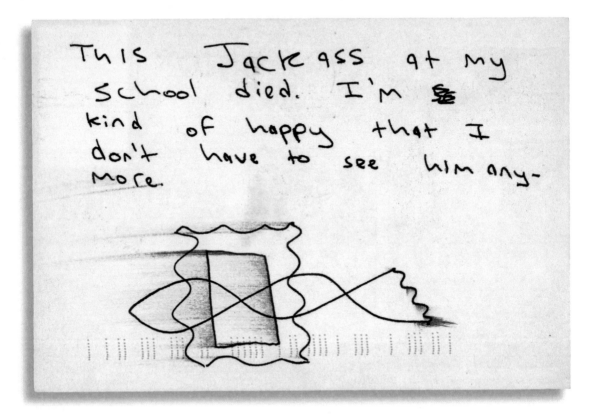

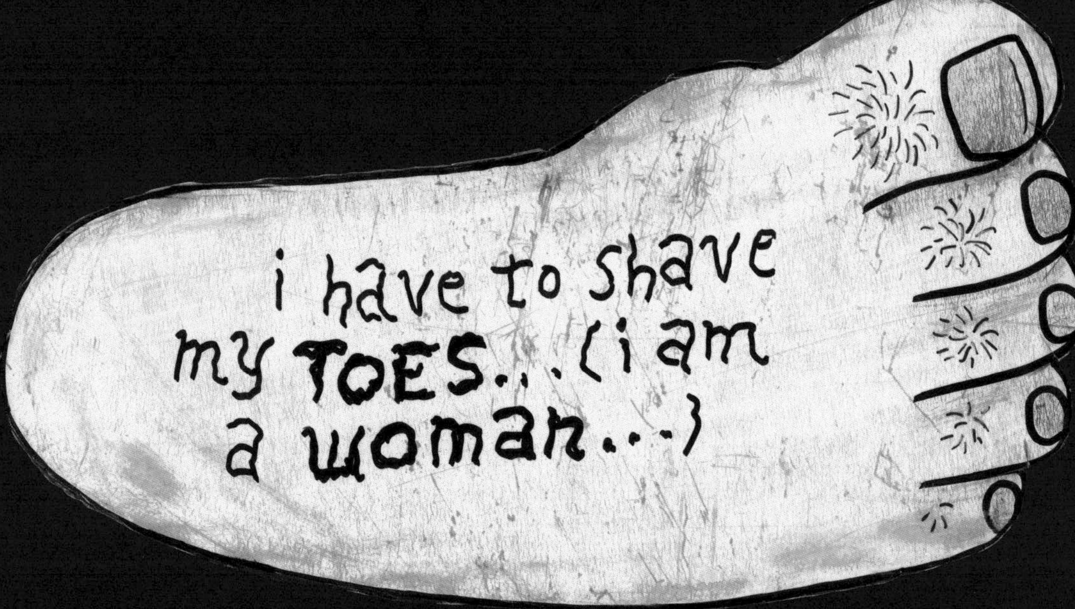
i have to shave
my TOES... (i am
a woman...)

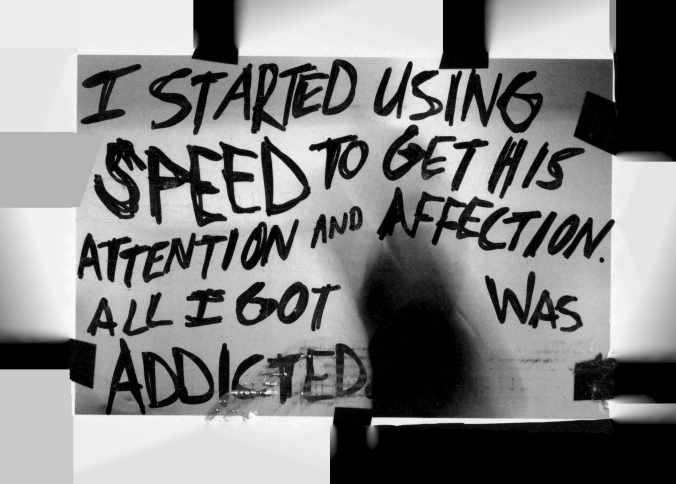

MY MOM
KILLED MY
DAD,
LONG BEFORE
HE KILLED
HIMSELF.

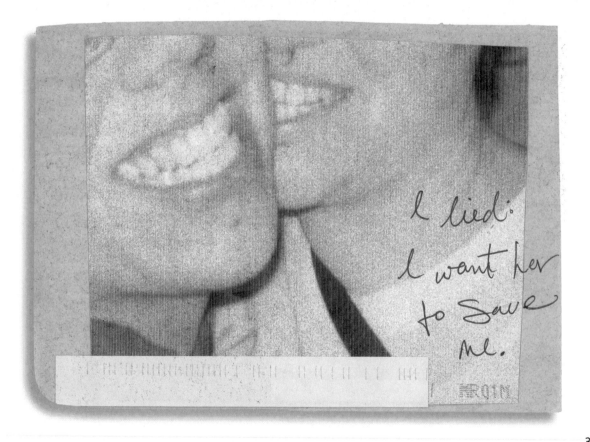

All the time we've spent in love...
I didn't really know you loved me
until you danced with me...in public...
even though you didn't know how.
Even if I never get that chance again,
it was worth the awkward fumbling
to know that what you've said is true.

313

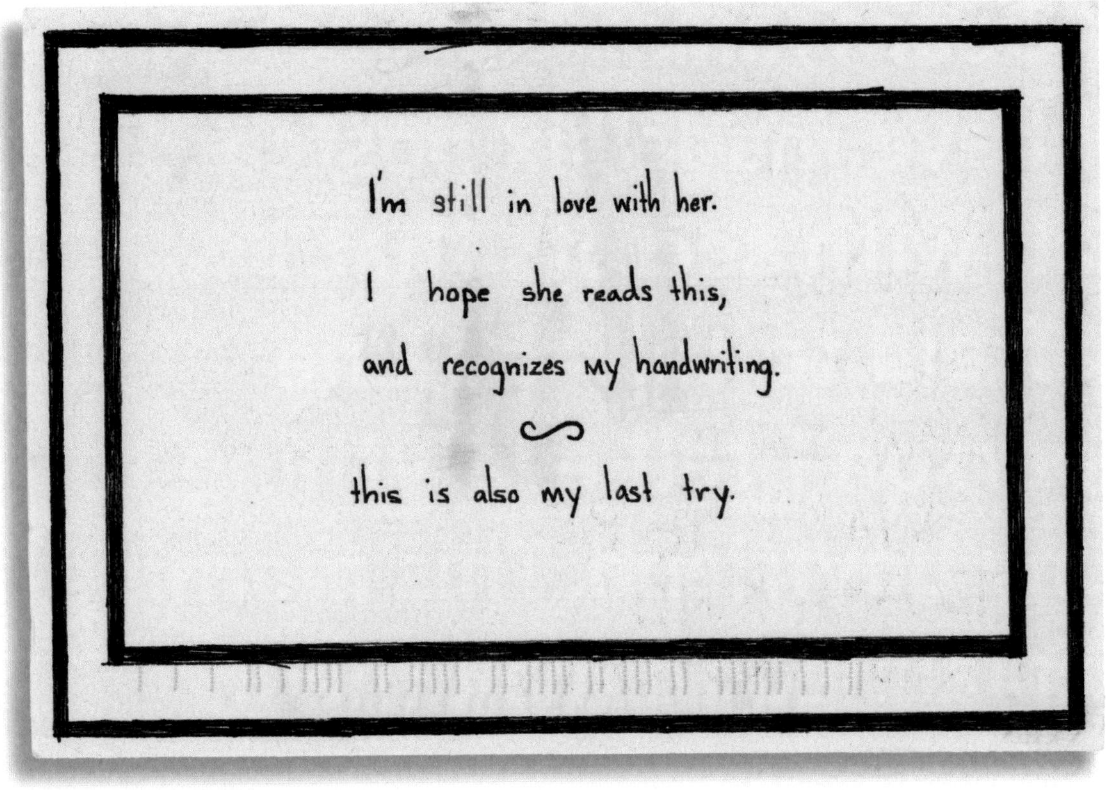

I'm still in love with her.

I hope she reads this,

and recognizes my handwriting.

∽

this is also my last try.

"Dear Frank,
I have made six postcards,
all with secrets that I was
afraid to tell the one
person I tell everything to,
my boyfriend. This morning
I planned to mail them,

but instead I left them on the pillow next to his head while he was sleeping. Ten minutes ago he arrived at my office and asked me to marry him. I said yes."

—Canada

I FAKED SORROW

at my Dad's **Funeral**, When I, in fact, was Selfishly **Happy** I didn't have to wipe his **BUTT** anymore.

319

I'M Sorry,
We were Young, I think about
-- and Regret -- it every Day.

Sharon:
innocent freckle-faced red-haired
good Sharon:
I was a vicious vengeful
compulsive BRUTE to you at
school.
30+years on- Now I'm very sorry

I'm known as the "funny" one, but I don't crack jokes to make people smile.

It's because I fear feeling their sadness.

This way up

WITHOUT SUFFERING, THERE IS NO COMPASSION.

During college I worked at a restaurant where we took turns running the cash register. I stole probably about $5,000.00 over those 4 years. Most of that money went towards the year I spent backpacking around Europe. I had a great time.

I only smoke
Pall Mall Cigarettes
so I can
remember you
forty times
a day...

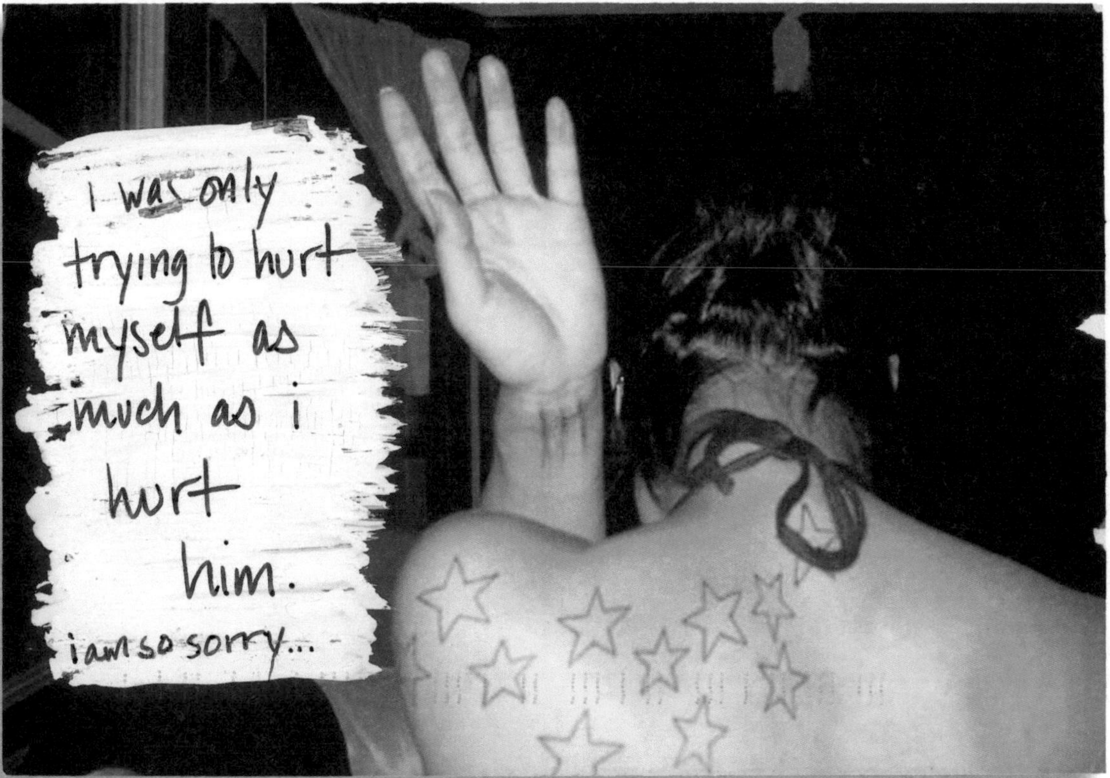
i was only
trying to hurt
myself as
much as i
hurt
him.
i am so sorry...

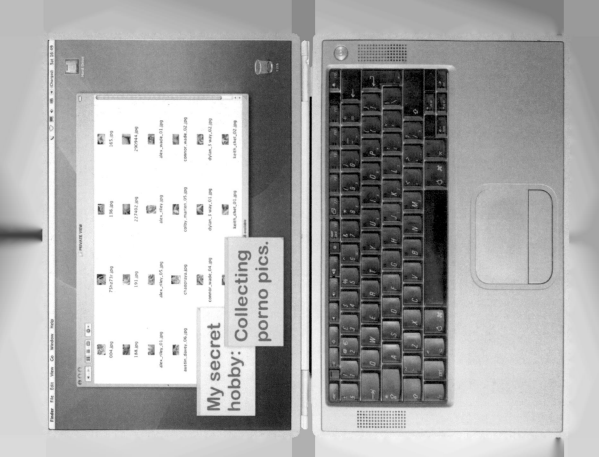

My husband doesn't know that I know he has porn on our computer...
OR
that I masturbate to it!

My boss is Black, I've dated Black men, I have friends of all ethnic backgrounds and I am a minority, too a minority, too ...but I'm still a Racist.

BROOKLYN NY 11?5?
PM
02 JUN
2005

3c USA 3c USA USA 23

THANK
YOU!

Post Secret
13345 copper Ridge Road
Germantown, Maryland
          20874-3454

Back: I burn my father's porn when he's not home.

i'd rather get SKiN CaNCeR than be PALE

I try to be
CONTENT...
but the truth is
life would be so much easier
if I were pretty.
Me→
HONOLULU HI 968
PM

I STOLE YOUR DUCK AND TOOK HIM TO SAN FRANCISCO

335

the night he died he tried to call me...when I saw it was him, I didnt answer.

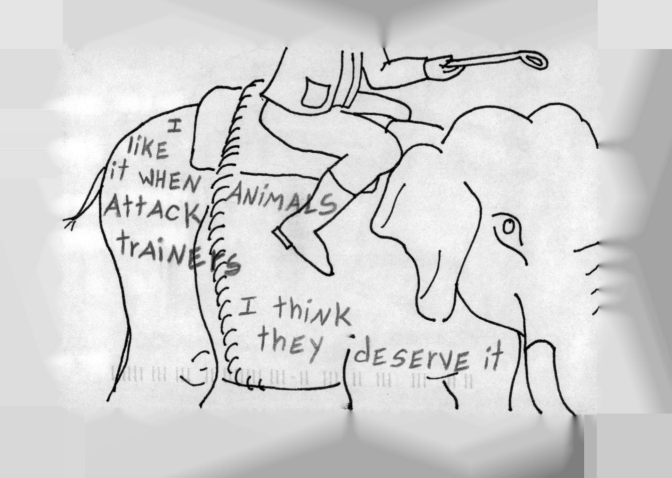

I SENT MYSELF FLOWERS ON VALENTINES DAY SO PEOPLE AT WORK WOULD THINK I WAS DATING SOMEONE!!!

Daisy
I love you

White rose
I can not

...not
...get me

Language of bouquets

Narciss...
...hen can I s...
agai...

...er me

Yellow Rose
Contentment

Pink: Yes!

Write the name under the bouquet desired

Edelweiss
Write soon

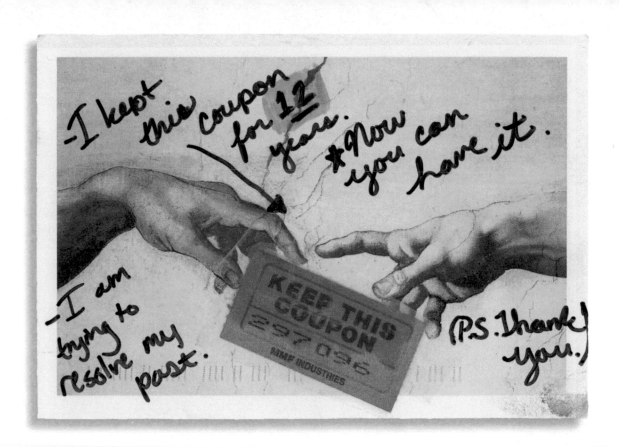

341

I need to change.

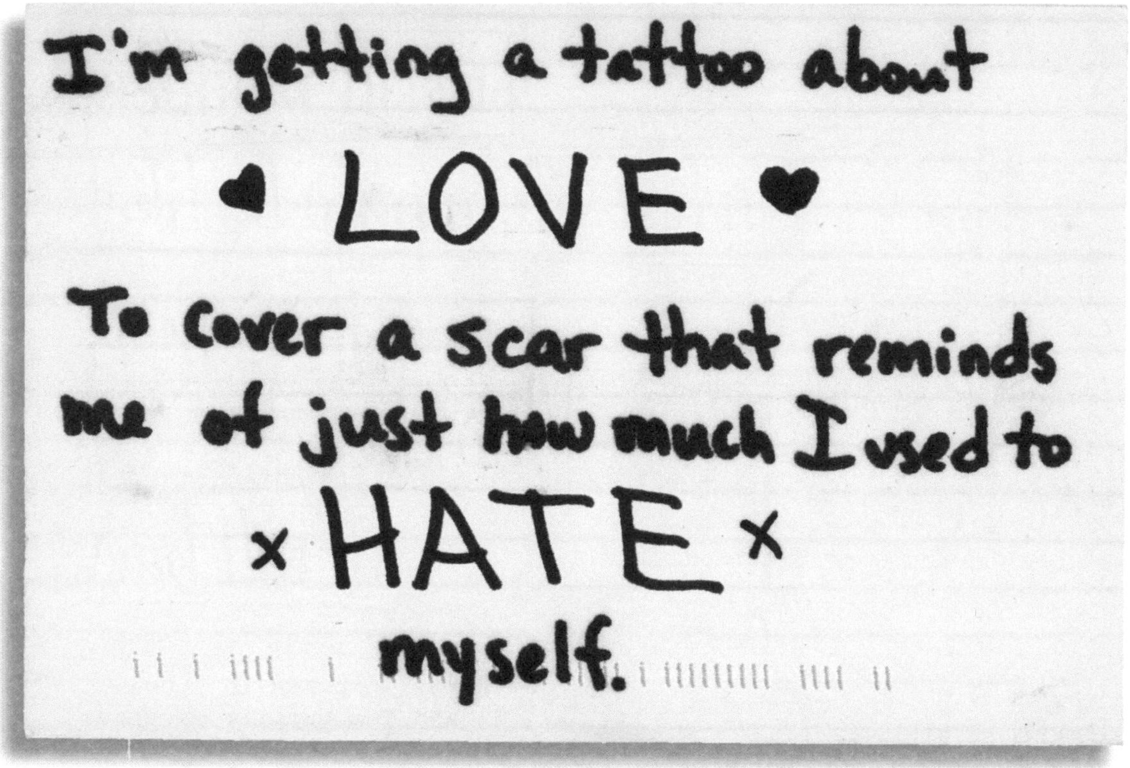

I'm getting a tattoo about

♥ LOVE ♥

To cover a scar that reminds
me of just how much I used to

× HATE ×

myself.

I still wonder what life would be like if I'd just had the *courage* to tell her

We haven't spoken in 5 years and I'm happily married

344

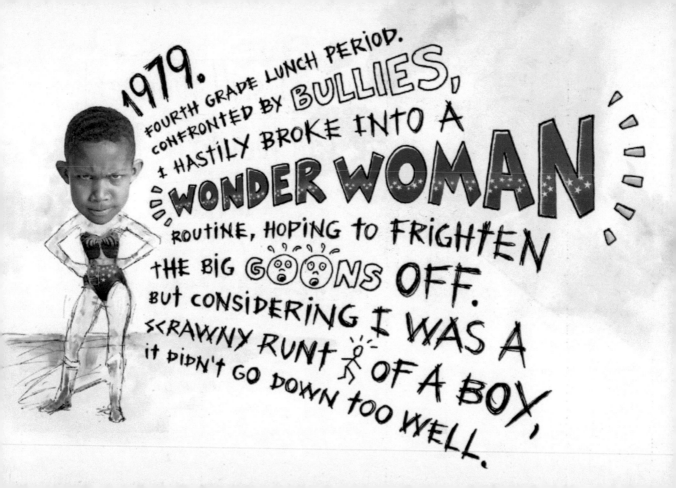

I change my hair so often to make
up for the fact that I won't be
able to change who I am.

I intentionally make myself nearly a half an hour late to work every morning so I can ride the bus with the hot bus driver, in hopes that we may make eye

contact in the rear view mirror and perhaps start a conversation. I think up hundreds of opening lines as I let buses pass me by, but when he opens the doors and smiles brightly and looks at me with his beautiful sparkling blue eyes I find myself tongue twisted. I end up burying my head inside a book. Maybe he'll read this someday......

I TRASHED MY PARENTS HOUSE TO LOOK LIKE I HAD HAD A PARTY WHILE THEY WERE OUT OF TOWN...
...SO MY MOM WOULD THINK I HAD FRIENDS:

I hope there is a
heaven.

(and I hope you're
there.)

352

Psst, Here's a secret...
Your last mortal thought
will be, "why did I take
so many days — just like
today — for granted?"

I know that sending in a stupid postcard to share a secret with a bunch of strangers won't do a damn thing to change the daily loneliness and unhappiness in my life.

And I sent this anyway.

I bought a bunch of postcard
stamps to use for Post Secret

but I used them to write

to my friends instead.

I like to believe that whenever a painful secret ends its trip to my mailbox, a much longer personal journey of healing is beginning—for all of us.

—Frank

PostSecret has earned several awards, including Blog of the Year and four Webbys for best Net-Art. Frank has appeared on *The Today Show*, CNN and Fox News among other programmes to talk about the project. He lives in Maryland with his wife and daughter, and continues to travel to college campuses and lecture about PostSecret; his website www.PostSecret.com receives over 5 million visitors every month. Two PostSecret art exhibits continue to travel internationally every month.

By Frank Warren

PostSecret: Extraordinary Confessions from Ordinary Lives

My Secret: A PostSecret Book

The Secret Lives of Men and Women: A PostSecret Book

A Lifetime of Secrets: A PostSecret Book

SHARE A SECRET

You are invited to anonymously contribute a secret to a group art project. Your secret can be a regret, fear, betrayal, desire, confession or childhood humiliation. Reveal *anything* - as long as it is true and you have never shared it with anyone before.

Steps:
    Take a postcard, or two.
    Tell your secret anonymously.
    Stamp and mail the postcard.

Tips:
    Be brief – the fewer words used the better.
    Be legible – use big, clear and bold lettering.
    Be creative – let the postcard be your canvas.

SEE A SECRET
www.postsecret.com

place
postage
here

PostSecret
13345 Copper Ridge Rd
Germantown, Maryland
20874-3454